PRAIRIE
MURDERS

PRAIRIE MURDERS

Mysteries, Crimes and Scandals

PETER B. SMITH

VICTORIA · VANCOUVER · CALGARY

Heritage House Publishing Company Ltd.
#108 – 17665 66A Avenue
Surrey, BC V3S 2A7
www.heritagehouse.ca

Heritage House Publishing Company Ltd.
PO Box 468
Custer, WA
98240-0468

Library and Archives Canada Cataloguing in Publication
Smith, Peter B., 1946 –
     Prairie murders: mysteries, crimes and scandals / Peter B. Smith. — 1st Heritage House ed.

ISBN 978-1-894974-71-4

1. Murder — Prairie Provinces — History. I. Title.
HV6535.C32P7 2009   364.152'309712   C2009-900123-3

Originally published 2005 by Altitude Publishing Canada Ltd.

Library of Congress Control Number: 2009920303

Series editor: Lesley Reynolds.
Cover design: Chyla Cardinal. Interior design: Frances Hunter.
Cover photo: Jarek Szymanski/iStockphoto. Interior photos: Glenbow Archives, NA-3282-1, page 41; *Calgary Sun*, page 81.

Printed in Canada

Heritage House acknowledges the financial support for its publishing program from the Government of Canada through the Book Publishing Industry Development Program (BPIDP), Canada Council for the Arts, and the province of British Columbia through the British Columbia Arts Council and the Book Publishing Tax Credit.

The Canada Council | Le Conseil des Arts
for the Arts | du Canada

BRITISH COLUMBIA
ARTS COUNCIL
Supported by the Province of British Columbia

This book has been produced on 100% post-consumer recycled paper, processed chlorine free and printed with vegetable-based inks.

12 11 10 09   1 2 3 4 5

To all my secret sources.
Right on.

Contents

Prologue

IT WAS A SHOCKING MOMENT *of revelation for the head of the homicide unit. His detectives had hunted this suspect for months after an old man in Calgary had disappeared and the blood-splashed interior of his house made it obvious he'd been murdered right there, then taken away and dumped. Staff Sergeant George Rocks, head of Calgary city homicide unit, told me how he'd waited for this moment when his lead detectives would caution and charge suspect Raymond Tudor with murder: "When we caught him, he's wearing the victim's watch, he's got blood on his cowboy boots, he's got blood on his clothing, he's got the victim's car, the victim's credit cards and keys, and the victim's wallet. He had the victim's guns, he had* the victim's liquor, and he had the victim's cigarettes. The evidence was overwhelming."

Rocks recalled how he was monitoring, on close-circuit television, the vital moments in the interview as two homicide detectives, Calvin Johnson and Brent Refvik, were spelling out to Tudor that he was being charged with murder.

Tudor suddenly looked at them with a grin on his face and said, "Do you know, you are wearing the ugliest ties I've ever seen."

Rocks couldn't believe his ears: "I sat there thinking, 'this is insane, absolutely insane. This man's just been told he's being tagged with a murder and he's more interested in joking about the detectives' ties.'"

It gave Rocks an instant insight into the man they'd been hunting. "I thought, 'this man is an animal. This guy has no emotions. This is a cold-blooded killer. He has no value for human life. None.'"

As Rocks finished relating this moment, he added, "By the way, Tudor had one thing right. They were really terrible ties!"

CHAPTER

1

Vanishing Act

IT WAS AN ODD REQUEST. The Calgary Police Service Crime Stoppers Unit needed an elderly actor who could convincingly play a dead body. The police couldn't turn to modelling agencies because they always sent handsome young men. In the end, a cop offered the unit his dad, Howard Owen. Owen made an excellent corpse, though he later said it had turned his stomach to lie on the floor exactly where an elderly man had been murdered.

Six weeks earlier, on April 29, 1994, a killer had bludgeoned to death retired railwayman Ardie Turner, 77. The murderer had left the body lying on the kitchen floor of the old man's rented tumbledown farmhouse on Highway 797 in the prairie village of Langdon, southeast of Calgary.

With the murder still unsolved after six weeks, the Calgary RCMP had opted for a TV re-enactment in the hope that television coverage would spark new information from the public. The crime scene was now bustling with a fake corpse, a fake killer, a camera operator and a film director. It looked like robbery had been the motive, because Ardie's meagre pension was missing along with his camera. And, most importantly, his beloved old truck had been driven away by his attacker.

Ardie had been a sociable bachelor who spent his days driving his 1977 GMC El Camino to visit numerous friends in the surrounding villages of Dalemead and Carseland to the south and Beiseker to the north, where he'd always be invited in for coffee and a chat. That old truck was the only promising lead police had found. Two days after the murder, it was discovered abandoned in the parking lot of one of Calgary's busiest shopping malls—Chinook Centre—where it had been dumped by the killer. But days of intense forensic examination failed to yield a single clue, and the murder remained unsolved. Then another elderly man disappeared.

Robert William (Bill) Vomastic, 68, was living on his own in his southwest Calgary home. He had seemed perfectly fine when his son, James, visited him on the evening of Thursday, August 24, 1995. One of his dad's friends, Ray Tudor, arrived while James was there, and the three of them talked while Ray helped himself to old Bill's rye and cigarettes. After a while, James set off for home, leaving the two men still chatting.

12

The next day, Bill didn't show up for an appointment with his son. On Saturday, James picked up his sister, Sharon, and they both went over to see why their dad hadn't turned up. What they found in old Bill's home had them so worried they immediately went to the District 2 police station to report their dad missing. They already feared the worst had happened.

Some of the furniture had been moved, obviously by someone trying to hide a large bloodstain on the floor. A few things were missing, including Bill's car, and there was a ridiculous note that read, "Gone fishing in Montana. Dad." This was something their dad would never have done, and the note wasn't even in his handwriting. If it was supposed to allay their fears and explain where he was, it produced exactly the opposite reaction. It aroused their suspicions and sent them straight to the police. Officers didn't like what they heard from the distraught brother and sister and soon homicide detectives were at the house. Now things began to happen fast.

No sooner had the description of old Bill's white 1991 Ford Crown Victoria car, licence PZZ 399, been circulated to every officer on duty throughout the city than police spotted it being driven in the southeast section of Calgary. When police stopped the car, three people leaped out and scattered in different directions. The pursuing officers managed to chase down and catch the driver. Well, if it wasn't Ray Tudor! And here he was driving Bill's car, wearing Bill's watch and carrying Bill's wallet, with Bill nowhere to be found.

Calgary's forensic specialists found a lot of blood in Bill's house, and they already knew that Tudor had been alone with the victim just before he disappeared. Even if he didn't have Vomastic's body, the head of the homicide unit, Staff Sergeant George Rocks, was sure that old Bill had been murdered and here was the killer. Raymond (Ray) John Tudor, born August 29, 1953, of no fixed address, was charged with the second-degree murder of Robert William Vomastic.

But the anguish for Vomastic's son and daughter was in no way eased by knowing a suspect had been charged. They desperately needed their father's body found if they were to have any chance of closure in their lives. Tudor was saying nothing and public appeals for Calgarians to look out for the body bore no results.

Homicide detectives appealed to the public to keep their eyes open for specific items missing from Bill's home—a set of dark green cloth curtains and a white floral-pattern bedspread. Police were convinced these items had been wrapped round Bill's body, which was then carried to his car and later dumped somewhere.

This time their appeals were successful. A local resident who was walking near the village of Dalemead, 20 kilometres southeast of Calgary, found the bloodstained curtains. The discovery served to concentrate the search for the body in that area. On the evening of September 22, almost a month after the murder, a pheasant hunter's dog found a shallow grave containing Bill Vomastic's decomposed remains in a patch of heavy brush about 30 kilometres southeast of Calgary, near Carseland, Alberta.

This was especially interesting news to the RCMP investigators who still had Ardie Turner's unsolved murder on their files. Here were two murders of old men. Both had apparently been killed in their own homes, and in each case the killer had stolen valuables from inside the house, then driven off in the victim's vehicle. Ardie Turner's home was on the prairies southeast of Calgary, and now Vomastic's body had been found dumped in the same area. What's more, Bill Vomastic had known Ray Tudor, his suspected killer, for years. RCMP inquiries soon revealed that Tudor was also an acquaintance of Ardie Turner. Ardie had used him as a mechanic for work on his truck.

A bombshell breakthrough in the spring of 1996, two years after Turner's murder, made the difference. An eyewitness came forward to say he'd dropped a man off on the night of the killing right near the victim's house. The man he dropped off was Ray Tudor. On May 31, 1996, Tudor was charged with the first-degree murder of Ardie Turner, and a year later the Turner slaying was the first of the two trials to begin at the Calgary Court of Queen's Bench.

The first shock of the trial came when the accused killer's own brother, Roger Tudor, appeared for the prosecution. He told the jury that old Ardie Turner was like a father to him, and that he had arranged the old man's funeral and was pleased to have done so. He claimed to have no clue that his drunkard brother had anything to do with the murder.

Alberta's deputy chief medical examiner, Dr. Lloyd Denmark, said Turner had been smashed over the head 14 times with something like a tire iron. The sheer brutality of the murder made a significant impact on the jury. The jury also heard of a weird episode with a man who first contacted police under the alias of Zorro 23, better known to his friends as Nollind Dodd. Zorro demanded $50,000 to tell what he knew, ostensibly to help hide him in a witness protection program. He eventually became the Crown's star witness, giving evidence that nailed down the case against Raymond John Tudor.

Dodd claimed that Ray had called him on the night of the murder and had asked Dodd to drive him out to Langdon, near Turner's home. After they arrived, they sat around in the car, sinking a six-pack of beer and throwing the cans out of the windows. Then Ray, who was dressed in heavy, dark clothing "just like a burglar," got out of the car and ordered Dodd to drive away.

The jury immediately saw the significance of the testimony. Ray obviously wouldn't need Dodd to hang around and drive him home later, because he knew that if his murderous plan worked out he'd have a vehicle—Turner's beloved old truck. Dodd also told the jury that early the next day Ray had them race back out near Turner's home to pick up all the beer cans, so police wouldn't find their fingerprints on them. The jury saw this as damning testimony. Tudor was retrieving the incriminating evidence of his crime before Turner's body had even been found.

Chief Crown Prosecutor Bruce Fraser outlined a simple scenario. Tudor, knowing old Ardie Turner was alone and vulnerable, went there to rob and kill him. Tudor beat him to death, robbed him of his paltry pension money, took the keys to his truck and simply drove away. Defence lawyers Sandy Park and Jim Lutz applied to the judge, Justice David Wilkins, to have the charges thrown out because, they submitted, there wasn't a "scintilla of evidence" that Tudor had planned the murder. Nor was there any direct evidence that he was ever inside Turner's house.

The judge dismissed their application and put the case in the hands of the jury, who saw it as clearly as Fraser had portrayed it. On June 27, 1997, after deliberating for 14 hours, the jury found Raymond John Tudor guilty of first-degree murder, leaving Justice Wilkins with no alternative but to impose the mandatory life sentence with no parole for 25 years. Tudor, whose last act before leaving the court-room was to sneer at the jury and shake his head, was only in prison a few months before he was back in the Court of Queen's Bench to face the second murder rap.

This time it was before a judge alone—a different judge— but the facts outlined by the new Crown prosecutor, Jerry

Selinger, were *déjà vu* to anyone who knew the case. Selinger pointed out that Ray Tudor knew old Bill Vomastic and that while visiting Vomastic's home he murdered him. He then robbed him of his cash, his wallet, his booze, his cigarettes, his gold watch and his gun collection, and then drove off in his car.

But Tudor had added a few refinements to his second killing. This time he hid the body, hoping it would never be found, and left a "Gone fishing in Montana" note. He assumed everyone would think old Bill was away fishing and wouldn't even realize a crime had been committed.

The two days after the murder had been party time for Tudor. First, with amazing bravado, he drove his victim's car to Calgary's courthouse, parked and went in to face a completely unrelated charge. Later, he uncharacteristically took his friends on a drinking spree at various bars, liberally splashing out his new-found cash, getting ever more drunk. Only three days earlier, he'd been picking up cans because he didn't have two coins to rub together. He even paid the bar tabs of his friends using the dead man's credit card and identity. The drinking binge didn't stop until cops cut it short by nabbing Tudor.

The judge heard evidence of the brutality inflicted by Tudor. Dr. Denmark, the same medical examiner who'd seen Tudor's handiwork on the skull of Ardie Turner, testified to what he found on Bill Vomastic's decomposed body. Seven lunging stab wounds in the back had killed him, some so powerful they had severed his ribs. They were almost certainly inflicted by Vomastic's own First World War bayonet, which had been part of his weapons collection. Denmark proved the murderous attack by matching the seven holes in the shirt Vomastic was wearing with the seven holes in his body.

One of Tudor's friends testified that Ray had turned up at his home in the early hours soon after Vomastic was slain, heavily blood-splattered and very drunk, in what turned out to be old Bill's car. Tudor's story was that he had been beaten up and bloodied in a bar brawl in Montana. The friend didn't believe it, and neither did the judge.

On December 3, 1997, Justice Robert Cairns found Raymond John Tudor guilty of the second-degree murder of Robert William Vomastic and gave him a second life sentence, with no parole for 20 years. Outside the courthouse, Vomastic's daughter, Sharon, who'd endured the anguish of her father's murder and the prolonged agony of not knowing where his body had been dumped, remarked on the verdict. "I think justice has been served . . . I think the only way that Tudor is going to come out of jail is in a pine box . . . and I hope that's the case."

That may have been the intention of the law and it was certainly Sharon's fervent hope. But that wasn't how Ray Tudor saw it. He had escaping on his mind even before the trials had started. The judge heard during the Vomastic trial that back in 1995 Tudor had been held in a Calgary forensic unit on psychiatric remand while charged with Vomastic's murder. He was sporting an arsenal of escape tools: two hacksaw blades, two flat-ended screwdrivers and a fantastic homemade handcuff key fashioned from the plastic insides of a pen. A guard tried it on a pair of handcuffs and was shocked to find it worked. In a later search of Tudor's cell, authorities found a 34-metre-long string of bedsheets knotted together and noticed that the caulking around his window frame had been dug out. "You don't have to be a rocket scientist to figure out why he had those tools," said Justice Cairns. He ruled that they were proof of a planned breakout, thwarted by alert staff and a tip from a fellow inmate at the unit.

Tudor began his two life sentences in the maximum-security Edmonton Institution prison, but in 2000 two notable events took place. On the appeal of the Ardie Turner trial, Tudor's first-degree murder conviction was reduced to second-degree murder, and his sentence of life with no parole for 25 years was reduced to life with no parole for 20 years. Then he was transferred to the medium-security Drumheller Institution northeast of Calgary, where guards saw his health deteriorating badly and where he was clearly aging fast.

Although he was only 47 years old, his beard grew long and grey, aging his haggard face. He developed increasingly bad shaking and trembling symptoms and appeared to be suffering from advanced Parkinson's disease. His condition worsened almost daily. By 2002, he was a trembling old man, a doddery senior with a debilitating and uncontrollable stutter. Tudor was no longer considered an escape threat. Except that on March 26, 2002, he escaped—clean as a whistle!

In previous breakouts, prison guards had established exactly how the escapees had wriggled out. There was one notable breakout where the escapee was boxed into a crate by fellow prisoners and shipped out by truck to a downtown Drumheller store. But Tudor's Houdini-like escape left no clues. The Drumheller prison fence is topped by flesh-shredding razor wire, so he obviously didn't go that way. And none of the easily triggered ground or fence sensors were breached either.

But he was out, even if he was an almost helpless old man crippled with Parkinson's disease. People across Alberta were very uneasy—and none more so than the witnesses who had testified against him. He'd killed twice and had nothing to lose. They feared he'd come for them next. Case-hardened detectives also acknowledged the frightening prospect of his being unleashed into the community. Staff Sergeant Rocks of the Calgary homicide unit, who'd helped put Tudor behind bars, voiced this fear, "This guy is a cold-blooded killer. You have a very serious problem here."

Days passed. A few sightings of Tudor came in and were checked. Nothing. Then, after three weeks, prison authorities and police released a bombshell. Tudor was no doddery, helpless old man after all. It was a performance, all part of an elaborate hoax he'd spent months perfecting. He was as fit as the day he went inside. Tudor had cleverly transformed himself into this apparent human wreck as part of a brilliant escape plan—a plan that had an added advantage. "Immediately after he was out, he would have shaved off the long flowing beard and long greying hair . . . and lost the shakes," said Calgary detective Ryan Dobson.

Just as the prison description of the escapee hit the streets, telling people to watch out for a frail old man, he would have been looking decades younger with hands as steady as a rock.

The manhunt for Tudor went international. He was featured on the television series *America's Most Wanted*, after it was feared he could be on the lam south of the border. But not one worthwhile tip came in. It was seven weeks since he'd disappeared into thin air, leaving many frightened people looking over their shoulders for fear that he might be stalking them.

The stage was set for Tudor to make the biggest headlines of his life, this time right across Canada. He was finally captured where no one had thought to look for him. Not in the United States. Not stalking anxious witnesses in Calgary. Not threatening local residents in downtown Drumheller. Tudor was found in the ventilation duct above the workshop of the prison itself.

The story became more and more fantastic as increasingly incredible details poured out. Tudor had built himself trap doors, false walls and access holes throughout the ducting system over the prison's 7,616-square-metre industrial workshop. He'd been dropping down at night, stealing scraps from the kitchen to keep himself alive and then climbing back up into the pipework. In his hideaway in the ceiling they found a bottle of antacid tablets, some vitamin supplement pills, a homemade grappling hook, one can of coffee and some paint-thinner tins, which he'd used as his toilet. In his seven-week-long cat and mouse game, he had eluded infrared detectors and even sniffer dogs.

But two days before Tudor's capture, a prison guard reckoned he'd seen somebody moving under some machinery in the workshop. He thought it was Tudor, but knew he must be mistaken. Drumheller warden Floyd Wilson was taking no chances. Two days later, he called in a Calgary RCMP K-9 dog-handling team, as well as the Calgary Fire Department's Heavy Rescue Unit. Once the dogs had pinpointed where the fugitive was hiding in the pipes, the rescue co-ordinator, Mark Turik, put his men to work. They inserted a snake-eye camera into the pipe, and after some manipulating they saw their man. The firefighters, who were used to ripping roofs off cars to reach trapped accident victims, used their heavy tearing machinery to peel back the duct's metal skin until Tudor was visible through the hole. Calgary RCMP corporal Bill Hamilton grabbed the sawdust-covered and dishevelled Tudor. The seven-week hunt had ended.

So what possessed Tudor to hide there? George Rocks reckoned Tudor probably planned to stay up in the ceiling for several months until everyone forgot about him. Then he could drop down and slip out of the prison. "After all," said Rocks, "who would be looking inside a prison for a guy who'd escaped months before?"

Whatever the reason, Tudor sparked a furor in prisons across Canada. Duct openings and pipework access points were sealed up with locks and grates in jails across the nation. Inquiries were launched into why a double-murderer was in a medium-security prison in the first place and how any prisoner could live undetected in a jail for weeks.

Tudor, who was dubbed the Ductman of Drumheller and assured of a permanent place in prison folklore, was charged with being unlawfully at large. He was sent back to the maximum-security prison in Edmonton, where authorities vowed that he would never embarrass them with an escape.

The final word was left to warden Floyd Wilson at Drumheller Institution, who never did admit to being red-faced about having a prisoner loose in his prison pipes for seven weeks. After Tudor was dragged out of the ceiling, Wilson told the media, "I'm stimulated and excessively proud we have this individual in custody . . . proud he never exited the institution."

2

Deadly Ambush at Steep Creek

THE FIRST WORLD WAR WAS a bloodbath in Europe, and brave Canadian soldiers gave their lives all across France and Belgium. Many spent their last days lying in trenches under a hail of bullets and exploding shells. There was nothing they could do except fire at enemy soldiers.

Meanwhile, back on Canadian soil, two young French Canadians were doing whatever they could to avoid going off to war. Their efforts would lead to a number of vicious and cowardly murders and result in one of the largest manhunts ever seen in Saskatchewan.

What ended in bloodshed on a tiny prairie farm east of Prince Albert, Saskatchewan, began in the town of St. Hyacinthe, Quebec. It was there that Dr. Joseph Gervais, a mysterious character who dabbled in hard drugs and hypnotism, met two young men, Jean Baptiste St. Germain and Victor Carmel, while playing violin at a local dance. Gervais had a magnetic personality and easily persuaded the two young men to return home with him to Montreal. Later, in August 1917, the three men moved together to the heart of the Saskatchewan prairie.

Dr. Gervais and his two friends had formed a close and unusual bond. The doctor rented a farm in the Steep Creek area, 45 kilometres from the city of Prince Albert. The two young men worked for the doctor without pay, and the arrangement seemed to suit all three. St. Germain and Carmel were draft dodgers who were intent on avoiding the recently imposed conscription that would have sent them off to the western front of the war. Dr. Gervais had promised he'd hide them away where no one would find them, and they'd jumped at the chance. The doctor was pleased—he now had two handsome young men at his beck and call.

While Gervais lived in the log cabin farmhouse, he helped the younger men dig a cave in the side of the riverbank above the South Saskatchewan River. There the two lived, hidden away from the world. The cave was an elaborate underground construction, with main tunnels and escape tunnels, all properly shored up by timber supports. It also had secret exits linking it to the barn and stable up on the farm. Furnished with a stove, table, beds and chairs, it was so cleverly concealed—with heavy forest growth hiding its entrances—that no one in the community even knew it was there. Indeed, a great deal of planning had gone into its construction. Fearing that one day the Canadian military would come for them, St. Germain and Carmel had fashioned their cave in a way that would allow them to easily shoot anyone who approached.

Not much farming was ever carried out on the farm, but this strange trio always had a good supply of meat on the table. It was later discovered that they were raiding neighbouring farms at night, slaughtering cows and bringing home the beef. Despite this, the people in the community pretty well left Dr. Gervais and his seldom-seen companions alone.

Only one neighbour, Adolphe Lajoie, showed any real interest in what was going on at the recently rented farm. Unfortunately, Lajoie died when his farmhouse burned down one night. Authorities found his badly charred body in his bed with his pipe alongside him, a testimony to the tragic smoking accident that had taken his life. Or so they thought. Later, they would be forced to revisit this "accident."

On November 15, 1918, four days after the First World War ended, Prince Albert's deputy sheriff, James McKay, was sent to Dr. Gervais' farm on a routine matter. Gervais had neglected to pay for some horses he'd bought, and McKay had been assigned to seize them under a court order. The young officer was whistling as he got out of his Model-T Ford and crossed the farmyard to open the barn door.

Upon spotting the deputy sheriff, St. Germain and Carmel began to panic. Without warning, the two draft dodgers opened fire from inside their hideaway. McKay was badly wounded and slumped against a tree trunk to try to hold himself up. At this exact moment, Dr. Gervais arrived back at the farm—with a guest.

Gervais had been called away earlier that day to treat a neighbouring farmer's wife, who was in a coma brought on by Spanish influenza. The flu epidemic had already brought the spectre of death to many farms as it swept across the prairies. While tending his patient, the doctor had seen McKay's Model-T Ford pass the house, heading toward his farm. Concerned at the sight, he'd asked the sick woman's son, 20-year-old Joseph Desormeaux, to drive him back to his farm in the family's horse-drawn carriage. He'd said the matter was urgent.

Gervais and Desormeaux arrived at the top of the hill as the wounded McKay was still clinging to the tree trunk. Almost unable to believe his eyes, Desormeaux watched in horror as the doctor jumped into action and helped the two men finish off the deputy sheriff. They shot him in the hands to make him let go of the tree, and then forced him down the hill toward the river. When he struggled to get up, they shot him again, and he suddenly went still.

Desormeaux had just witnessed a murder. He was certain the three men would kill him next. Instead, they forced him to help dispose of the corpse. With Desormeaux' assistance, the killers tied McKay's body onto a plank of wood, weighed it down with stones and slid it under the ice of the South Saskatchewan River.

Still fearing for his life, Desormeaux watched as the doctor took charge of erasing all signs of the crime. Gervais chopped down the blood-smeared tree that McKay had clung to and burned it, together with all the bloodstained leaves on the ground. Then he carefully raked over the tracks made by McKay's Model-T Ford. When they were satisfied that not a trace of McKay was left (except his car), the three men returned to their dugout cave for a meal. They took Desormeaux with them and offered him food. The man couldn't eat. He wanted to go home, but they held him there, explaining they still had one more job for him to do.

The three killers then had Desormeaux use his team of horses to tow McKay's Model-T Ford a kilometre along the riverbank to a depression. There, the men rolled the car down the embankment, dismantled it and smashed the parts into small pieces, which they buried. It was as if McKay had never been on the property. There was now no car, no body and no crime scene. Just the severe inconvenience of one eyewitness.

Gervais turned to Desormeaux, who was sure his life was about to end. At gunpoint, the doctor told Desormeaux he was letting him go, but warned that they would kill him if he ever told another living soul about what he'd seen. Badly shaken and barely able to believe his luck, Desormeaux raced away from the farm and back to his home. His family later recounted that he had acted strangely upon his return. He had constantly paced up and down, chain-smoking, but had refused to tell his family what was troubling him.

When James McKay failed to return either to his office or his home back in Prince Albert, his friends and family became worried. What they feared most was that he'd suddenly taken ill with the dreaded influenza and was lying somewhere in desperate need of medical help. After four days of waiting and worrying, they started searching for him. It didn't occur to anyone that something criminal might have befallen him. The *Prince Albert Daily Herald* ran a tiny blurb on November 19 with little hint of any perceived danger. All it said was, "Sheriff's bailiff James McKay is missing since Friday. He left the city to go to the farm of Dr. Gervais in the Steep Creek district."

On that same day, Saskatchewan Provincial Police sergeant Stanley Kistruck was sent from Saskatoon to the Steep Creek district to look for McKay. He called at the Gervais farm on the pretext of checking whether the influenza epidemic had spread that far yet. He looked around the property, searching for clues, but McKay clearly wasn't there. Nor were there any signs that he ever had been there. Satisfied, Kistruck left.

As the sergeant was driving away, he met Joseph Desormeaux, who stopped him. It was the chance the young man had unconsciously been waiting for. Still in shock from what he'd seen four days earlier, Desormeaux had not breathed a word of the murder to anyone for fear that the killers would punish him. However, upon seeing Sergeant Kistruck, he realized it was time to come forward. The young man unburdened himself to the sergeant, spilling the whole grisly story. Desormeaux described how the three men had killed the deputy sheriff, dumped the body in the river, buried the car and forced him at gunpoint to help them. Shocked at the story, Kistruck immediately took Desormeaux to Prince Albert, where the latter was locked away in police protection—at his own request. Desormeaux had remembered vital details, including how there were underground tunnels, secret trap doors, defensive trenches and dugouts in and around a huge cave at the farm. He also told the authorities that the three men seemed to have an arsenal of weapons.

The next day, November 20, Kistruck personally led a provincial police posse to the farm, backed by a detachment of soldiers from Prince Albert as well as local men who had volunteered to help. At the farmhouse, Kistruck immediately arrested Dr. Gervais, who was still asleep in bed. Protesting his innocence, the doctor was taken back to Prince Albert while the soldiers began a search for St. Germain and Carmel. Thinking the pair might be hiding in the barn, the soldiers set it on fire, but did not smoke anyone out. The posse then realized that the two fugitives must have scurried underground through their tunnels into their main dugout.

As the soldiers began to search a thickly wooded area for an entrance to the dugout, Corporal Charles Horsley, a 22-year-old member of the 1st Depot Battalion, came across a wooden trap door in the ground and immediately tried to pry it open with his bayonet. Suddenly, shots rang out from underground. The two fugitives were shooting at Horsley through the wooden door. Wounded, he staggered back and turned to flee from the danger. Another shot was fired, and Horsley fell dead with a bullet through his lung.

A soldier who had been searching alongside Horsley then saw the two fugitives emerge from the dugout and disappear into the thick undergrowth. He got off one shot, but the pair managed to escape. When news of Horsley's death reached the Prince Albert jail, Dr. Gervais showed absolutely no surprise or remorse. He boasted that his two companions had designed and fortified the underground tunnels so well that they could kill 40 men without ever getting caught.

The soldiers retreated from the scene. Before they left, however, they blasted the dugout and its underground tunnels with dynamite, ensuring the fugitives could never use the elaborate system again. The small newspaper story about the missing deputy sheriff that previously had warranted only a paragraph was now the headline on the front page of the *Prince Albert Daily Herald*: TWO SLAIN AT STEEP CREEK.

For the next four days, the Steep Creek district became the focal point of one of the largest manhunts ever seen in

Saskatchewan. Police, soldiers and volunteers searched tirelessly for St. Germain and Carmel. Fear spread through farms in the area as families realized that two desperate and heavily armed men were on the loose in their midst.

Late on November 23, two rough-looking strangers who claimed they were hunting turned up at a farmhouse located about 10 kilometres east of Prince Albert. They asked the man of the house, Charlie Young, for some water, and Young obliged. Before dawn the next morning they called again, this time asking for and getting food. The pair explained that it was too cold for hunting and told Young that they had decided to return to Prince Albert. But Young was suspicious of the story. He knew there was a manhunt underway in the area and thought he ought to warn police about the strangers. Afraid that the pair was hanging around outside his home and might hear him make the call, he waited all day Saturday until he was sure they were gone. Finally, at 11 o'clock that night, he telephoned the police with his information.

Early in the morning of November 25, the manhunt shifted to Charlie Young's farm, where the posse surrounded a haystack. Minutes later, Jean Baptiste St. Germain and Victor Carmel, who'd both been hiding inside the haystack, were arrested. The *Prince Albert Daily Herald* published a dramatic account of the capture that ended the manhunt. It reported that the leaders of the posse had fired shots in the air and had then shouted to the two fugitives to come out with their hands up or the police would riddle the haystack with bullets. Out they came. "They were in a state almost bordering upon collapse from hunger and exposure and were taken without a struggle," wrote a Prince Albert reporter. Both men had handguns with them when they surrendered, and they told the posse where the police could find the stolen rifles they'd hidden in the woods.

Later that day, after they'd been manacled and secured in the Prince Albert jail, St. Germain and Carmel confessed to being draft dodgers and to having shot and killed both the deputy sheriff and the soldier. For the first time, the police heard the chilling details from the lips of the killers: how James McKay had been whistling happily to himself, completely unaware of any danger when they had both opened fire on him; how he'd clung to a tree, still trying to stand; and how they had shot him repeatedly until he finally collapsed and died. Then they told the police how they'd dumped McKay in the South Saskatchewan River. Divers were sent to the river to search under the ice, but they couldn't find McKay's body. In fact, it's never been found to this day.

As the investigation continued, another startling claim was made. Dr. Gervais revealed to police that one of the young men, Victor Carmel, was responsible for the murder of Adolphe Lajoie, the Steep Creek farmer who had been curious about the trio. Gervais asked an officer if the police remembered a fire at a farmhouse where a farmer had been burned to death. They remembered the incident very well. Investigators had found Adolphe Lajoie's pipe alongside his body and concluded the farmer had caused the fire himself by smoking in bed. But Gervais' next statement stunned them all. The doctor told them that investigators had found the pipe beside the bed because that's where Victor Carmel had planted it to make the death look like an accident. Carmel had shot Lajoie in the head and placed his body in the bed, his pipe next to it. According to Gervais, Carmel had committed the murder because he'd felt that Lajoie knew too much about him and St. Germain and might go to the authorities. Then, just before Carmel had set the farmhouse ablaze, he'd stolen all the guns he could find. These guns provided the bulk of the killers' arsenal.

Astounded that the fire investigators had missed critical evidence, the police exhumed Lajoie's body. They found the telltale bullet hole in the late farmer's skull. Then, to cement Gervais' claim, Victor Carmel confessed to the killing.

All three men were charged with the murder of James McKay. The trial before a jury of 12 men at the Court of King's Bench in Prince Albert was delayed until May 10, 1919, because the deadly Spanish flu epidemic was still ravaging the prairies. Dr. Joseph Gervais, then 41, based his defence on a plea of insanity. His lawyers pointed out that while awaiting trial, he had spent most of his time in prison in floods of tears. He had even tried to hang himself with a knotted sheet, but the guards had saved him.

Meanwhile, Jean Baptiste St. Germain, 30, and Victor Carmel, 28, both claimed to have been under the hypnotic spell of the doctor and therefore were not responsible for their actions. But the jury didn't believe any of them.

All three were found guilty of murder and were sentenced to be hanged on September 17, 1919. When Chief Justice Brown came to sentencing, he unleashed one of the most emotional harangues ever heard in a court of law. In its annual report for 1919, the Saskatchewan Provincial Police Force quoted the judge's speech at length. This excerpt of his address to the prisoners reflects both revulsion at the murders they'd committed and society's disgust with draft dodgers:

> The crime of which you have been found guilty was so revolting that the posse of police and soldiers displayed British fair play in not shooting you on sight. Although France lay bleeding from one thousand wounds at the hand of a tyrannical, unscrupulous, and ruthless foe, and the spirit of France—which one would have thought would have appealed to you—called forth the sympathy and support of all heroic men within the Empire, you valued your own lives as more important than these things. You went into hiding. You dug yourselves into the ground. You conspired to defeat your country's purpose and shoot down like dogs the men who were trying to do their duty. Under the circumstances, simple justice would seem to demand that you go to the gallows in dishonour and shame, and suffer the extreme penalty of the law.

And they did. They had one rather routine stay of execution, but on October 17, 1919, a special scaffold was erected to take all three men at once. With one pull of a lever, Dr. Joseph Gervais, Jean Baptiste St. Germain and Victor Carmel all plunged downwards, their nooses snapped tight and they were hanged.

CHAPTER

3

Bootleggers
and Bloodshed

IF THEY'D HAD RACY, sensational tabloid weeklies in the
Crowsnest Pass in the early 1920s, it would have been
splashed across the front pages: "Gun-totin', bootleggin', raven-
haired Italian beauty shoots cop in back. Gets hanged."

In reality, rather more responsible journals recorded the
historical significance of the case with the headline: ALBERTA
HANGS ITS FIRST WOMAN MURDERER. And of course, they had
political commentators who expounded at length about
the significance of the police officer's murder as it related
to prohibition, the question of "foreigners" in Alberta's
population and the whole debate on capital punishment. It
was one hell of a story.

What led to a day of bullets and police bloodshed on a

Coleman village street in the Crowsnest Pass in 1922 really had its beginnings years earlier. When the whole world was embroiled in the First World War, the women of Alberta were also involved in a battle of their own. They were after two things—the vote and prohibition. They achieved both, winning the right to vote on April 19, 1916, and getting booze outlawed in Alberta on July 1, 1916, with full prohibition descending on the province on April Fool's Day, 1918.

You can't have prohibition in any society without a bootlegging industry being set up to defeat it. The number of thirsty throats doesn't dry up just because the law changes. And as bosses of every bootlegging operation quickly discover, you can't run an illicit booze industry without having a police force trying to dismantle your empire at every turn.

In the Crowsnest Pass in the 1920s, the Alberta Hotel in the village of Blairmore became "booze central." It was owned and run by the most notorious bootlegging baron of the whole Wild West, Emilio Picariello, a Sicilian known to everyone as Emperor Pic.

Look at Blairmore on a map of Alberta. It is tucked away in the southwest corner, almost off the map. But look at Blairmore in the big picture. It is centrally located if you are planning to run your bootleg booze north to Edmonton, west into British Columbia, east to Medicine Hat and south into Montana and Idaho. Which is exactly what Emperor Pic was doing, and doing very effectively, too. He acquired a fleet of big, powerful motor cars, McLaughlin Buicks, known as his "whisky specials," which could outrun most things on four wheels. His chief mechanic, who kept the fleet in raring-to-go condition, was Carlo Sanfidele, an Italian immigrant.

Among the growing wave of Italian immigrants who flooded into the Crowsnest Pass drawn by the promise of work in the coal mines, came the Constanzo family. They settled just over the British Columbia border in Fernie with their daughter, Filumena. The father ordered his 15-year-old girl to marry the much older Sanfidele, and the couple went south into the United States where Sanfidele tried and failed with various schemes to get rich quick. Upon encountering an immigration problem when trying to get back into Canada, he adeptly changed his name to Charles Lassandro. And when he encountered a constant problem with the pronunciation of Filumena's name, he ordered she be known instead as Florence. When they returned to Blairmore in the Crowsnest Pass, Charles Lassandro got his old job back as "wheel man" for Emperor Pic. His wife, who had started out as Filumena Sanfidele, was now known as Florence Lassandro.

Florence thrived on the exciting world of rum-running, fast cars, danger and adventure that the bootlegging runs through the Crowsnest Pass brought. She loved nothing better than to ride as the passenger on a booze run

Emilio Picariello, also known as "Emperor Pic"

with the Emperor, revelling in the knowledge that she had a .38 revolver nestled in her purse. Guns were commonplace among the Italians running the booze. In the two previous years, two Alberta Provincial Police (APP) officers had already been shot dead in the ongoing war against prohibition. The Emperor's bootleggers took Florence along as built-in insurance—they reckoned no cop would open fire on them with a woman in the car.

September 21, 1922, was to be a big day for the Emperor. He was personally escorting a convoy carrying a major consignment of his contraband liquor from Fernie, British Columbia, through the Crowsnest Pass to his hotel in Blairmore. He was in the lead McLaughlin Buick, with his son, Steve, behind him in the convoy driving the second whisky special. Unknown to Emperor Pic, word of his big booze run had spread. Such a juicy tip would earn a police informant a lucrative reward, and a well-placed rat had tipped off the cops. As the convoy approached the Alberta Hotel, officers of the APP force were already waiting to pounce.

But the ever-wary Emperor spotted the ambush waiting for his bootleggers and blasted the horn on his whisky special, the prearranged signal for his son in the next vehicle to spin on a dime and head his big McLaughlin back west, at least as far as the Alberta–British Columbia border, to safe ground. Meanwhile, the Emperor slewed his car across the road to block an immediate chase. Between Steve Picariello and the border, as he fled west, was the village of Coleman, but he'd soon be through there and into the pass. Back in Blairmore, Sergeant James Scott of the APP realized there was one last hope of intercepting the fugitive. He put through a telephone call to Constable Stephen Lawson in Coleman, warning him that the McLaughlin Buick was racing towards him and that it had to be stopped.

Lawson went out onto the highway and minutes later saw the whisky special barrelling straight at him. He put up his arm to stop it. But Steve Picariello had no intention of being taken and came close to knocking Lawson down as he raced through Coleman at breakneck speed. Lawson reacted instantly, firing at the tires of the speeding car as it fled west. A bullet hit the driver in the hand, but it didn't stop him. Determined, Lawson grabbed another officer. They sped after the Buick in a police car, only to suffer the frustration of a flat tire. That stopped them dead in their tracks. The Emperor's son reached the border and safety.

Only a panicky, garbled account of the shootout in Coleman reached the Emperor. He was told his son had been shot by a cop, but no one knew if Steve was alive or dead. Emperor Pic didn't know if his son had been captured by police or if he was lying bleeding to death beside the highway. What should have been a good rum-running day had been soured by a rat. The cops, especially the Coleman cop, had no damn business shooting his son. They were to blame, and they would pay. The Emperor, armed with his revolver, set off from Blairmore to Coleman to confront the police and find out what had happened to his son. Florence, who by this time had separated from her husband and was living as a housekeeper with the Emperor and his wife, Maria, insisted on going along—with her trusty, loaded .38 in her purse.

For the second time that day, Constable Lawson was

confronted by a McLaughlin Buick. Just before 7 p.m., the Emperor pulled up outside the little cottage that served as the police station in Coleman. Lawson, who lived in the police house with his wife and five children, walked out to meet the car with his nine-year-old daughter, Pearl, not far behind.

As Lawson leaned against the car, the Emperor's frustration and anger boiled over. He screamed at the officer for shooting his son. Then the Sicilian bootlegger pulled his gun and waved it at the cop. Unarmed, Lawson tried to get the Emperor in a headlock by reaching into the car, and they wrestled for control of the revolver. The gun went off several times, though neither man was hit.

Suddenly, Florence pulled out her .38 and shot Lawson in full view of his wide-eyed little girl. He had just turned from the car and was running back towards his house. He instantly dropped to the ground. Neighbours quickly ran out and carried Lawson into the little hospital next door to the police station, but he was beyond help. Before the doctors reached him, he was dead.

Eyewitnesses soon identified the Emperor as one of the shooters, and the next day the APP flooded the Blairmore and Coleman areas of the Crowsnest Pass to hunt the killers who had gunned down one of their own in cold blood. They soon captured Emperor Pic, who had fled to the hills behind Blairmore to hide. It wasn't long before the police were at Florence's door. Sergeant Scott, who'd telephoned to warn

Lawson what was coming his way when the ambush failed, confronted Florence. She said simply, "He's dead and I'm alive, and that is all there is to it."

Florence later gave a lengthier statement and said they hadn't intended to kill the police officer. She claimed that when the Emperor and the cop were wrestling for the gun in the car, the barrel swung towards her and she panicked and fired, fearing for her life. Police seized her .38 revolver and ballistics experts matched the fatal bullet to her gun.

It was impossible to find a neutral jury in the Crowsnest Pass, so the attorney general of the day, John Edward Brownlee, had the trial moved to Calgary. He attended the trial, though he left the prosecution itself to the distinguished Crown prosecutor Alexander A. McGillivray. The celebrated Calgary criminal lawyer, John McKinley Cameron, defended the two accused murderers.

It was an open-and-shut case from the beginning. McGillivray called on eyewitnesses who described the shooting of Lawson. He already had Florence's verbal statement to police, confessing that she shot the officer in the back. So much for her self-defence plea, which was as dead as Lawson by the time McGillivray had finished with it. And McGillivray brought on witnesses who'd heard the Emperor urging Florence to open fire. That made the Emperor as guilty as if he'd pulled the trigger himself. The jury came back with two guilty verdicts. There was no mention of mercy. Both Emilio Picariello and Florence Lassandro were sentenced to be hanged on February 21, 1923, at the Fort Saskatchewan Prison near Edmonton. The sentence of hanging came as a particularly nasty shock to Florence; nevertheless, she began to bide her time in jail with a secure inner feeling that society would never hang a woman. After all, no woman had been hanged anywhere in Canada that century, let alone a woman from a small town in the Crowsnest Pass, Alberta.

Defence lawyer John McKinley Cameron, who had precious little ammunition to fight with during the trial, fired off appeal after appeal in his battle to save the lives of the two condemned prisoners. He succeeded in getting their execution date put back by nearly three months to May, but the Supreme Court of Canada finally rejected his submissions. The gallows went up in the prison for the double hanging at 5 a.m. on May 2, 1923.

The Emperor went first, hanged promptly at 5 a.m. But this still didn't dent Florence's inner confidence that she would be spared at the last minute. Only when she was standing on the trap waiting for the hangman to fix the hood and noose did it suddenly seem to hit her that it really was going to happen.

There are various reports of what she said as that last-second realization sank in. In his book *A Dance with Death*, historian Frank W. Anderson records her words as, "Why do you hang me when I didn't do anything? Is there no one here who has any pity?" In her book *The Bootlegger's Bride*, Jock Carpenter has her saying, "I didn't hurt anyone ever. I will not forgive any of you for doing this to me." But after a few words from a priest who was providing her with spiritual strength in her final hours, she then said, "Father, I forgive . . . " It doesn't make much difference what she said; she was efficiently dispatched by Wakefield, the hangman, and just before 6 a.m. she was pronounced dead at the age of 22 years.

Now the case was in the realm of the commentators, analysts, armchair critics and historians who reflected on its meaning and interpreted its significance. Rumour mongers soon attached all manner of romantic notions to the plot. For instance, if this beautiful young woman was living in the Emperor's home, was she his secret mistress? And if she was, could it have been a romantically motivated expression of self-sacrifice that had made her confess, so the police would charge her and spare her man? Or were her affections aimed at the Emperor's son, Steve, who was more her own age? The trial threw no light on her romantic intentions towards either man, but that didn't stop the tongues from wagging.

Social commentators added their weighty analysis to the aftermath of the case by concentrating not on the cold-blooded gunning down of an unarmed police officer, but instead focussing on the hanged couple being Italian immigrants. During this turbulent period of the province's history, many Albertans had a perception that "foreigners" and immigrants, especially Italians, were a cause for distrust. They were seen as inherent lawbreakers.

A great number of Albertans considered it no accident that the province's major hotbed for bootlegging and rum-running was down in the Crowsnest Pass, where the greatest concentration of Italian immigrants was centred. Discrimination was so widespread that John McKinley Cameron, in defending Florence and Emperor Pic during the trial, reminded the jury that they must keep any such "anti-Italian" feelings out of their minds when considering whether the two were guilty or innocent.

One fact is without doubt. The whole case had an enormous impact on the prohibition debate in Alberta. Enforcing the prohibition law was next to impossible for the APP. Three of their officers had been killed in the last three years of the booze war. The cost was too high, and the results not rewarding enough. The anti-prohibition lobby, already strong in the southwest corner of Alberta, found more support from all over the province. In late 1923, the prohibition law was rescinded and booze flowed freely and legally through the province again. Who knows what the women of the temperance movement must have thought of the irony—a bullet from the gun of a woman had wiped out all their hard work.

* * *

For decades, the case attracted historical authors, among them Frank Anderson, who visited the drama twice in *The Rum Runners* and *A Dance with Death: Canadian Women on the Gallows*; Jock Carpenter, in her book *The Bootlegger's Bride*; and James H. Gray, in his anthology *Talk to My Lawyer! Great Stories of Southern Alberta's Bar and Bench.*

More recently, the fate of Florence and the Emperor translated perfectly onto the Internet. The case is featured as one of Alberta's four biggest-ever trials on the Great Alberta *d* Law Cases website, which is compiled by the Heritage Community Foundation and funded by the Alberta Law Foundation. It was even turned into a radio drama. Finally, in 2003, the case spawned a highly acclaimed new opera called *Filumena* by John Estacio and John Murrell, staged by the Calgary Opera in association with the Banff Centre.

But of all the historians who have researched the case for posterity, the man who must have been closer to the feelings of both Florence and the Emperor than any other is Frank W. Anderson. Remarkably, he too had heard a judge sentence him to death and had spent time in the shadow of the hangman's noose. Frank was orphaned as a baby, grew up in foster homes, reform schools and jails, and when he was a teenager he was convicted of killing a prison guard and sentenced to death. But in his case, the sentence was commuted to life imprisonment and he spent 15 years behind bars.

How poignant a moment it must have been for Frank, who received the pity of the court in commuting his sentence, to record among the last words Florence said in those final seconds before the hangman's noose was put round her neck, "Is there no one here who has any pity?"

CHAPTER

4

"The Devil Made Me Do It"

DURING THE EARLY MORNING HOURS of Friday, January 29, 1932, a fierce blizzard blew in across the Manitoba prairies from the northeast, plunging temperatures to –20°C. The tiny railway town of Elma, about 100 kilometres east of Winnipeg, suffered a whiteout in the grip of the blizzard. But at 6:30 a.m., when Nellie Kachur looked out her farmhouse window, she could clearly see flames shooting up from the next farmhouse. The Sitars' house was on fire! Nellie's friends, Martin Sitar, 66, and his wife, Josephine, 55, had lived there for 35 years, and 5 of their 10 children still lived there with them.

Nellie immediately woke her son Mike and told him about the fire. The pair dressed frantically, then raced to the neighbouring farmhouse to see if they could help. They were expecting to find the Sitar family outside, and Nellie was hoping that she and Mike could help them fight the blaze. As they ran the last few paces, they were shocked at how fast the fire had spread. The farmhouse was a mass of blood-red flames roaring from the roof and windows. Thick black smoke enveloped the entire building. Not one person was outside.

It looked like Nellie and Mike were the only lifeline for the Sitars, who were presumably still inside the inferno. Mike acted fast, racing straight to the front door to get in. Strangely, two heavy wooden posts had been jammed against the door from the outside. He couldn't move them, and that meant he couldn't get in through the door. More horrifying was the realization that no one inside could get out.

Mike raced over to the nearest window, but the choking smoke prevented him from even getting close. Frantically, he went back to the front door. This time he saw a heavy axe on the family's woodpile in the front yard. Smashing at the wooden posts, he succeeded in breaking them enough to wedge himself in through the front door. By this point, the main ceiling had crashed down, but Mike nevertheless fought his way in and found an unconscious Josephine Sitar. He managed to drag her outside, where he immediately noticed that she'd suffered a terrible head injury—perhaps from falling debris, he thought. Moments later, Josephine died.

As Mike braced himself to head back into the blazing home, his father, Andrew, arrived on the scene. Together, father and son plunged repeatedly into the collapsing inferno. It was a terrible ordeal for the two prairie farmers. First they brought out Martin Sitar, who was beyond their help. Then they managed to drag out the two youngest children. Jennie, aged seven, was terribly injured and burned and survived for only a short while. Paul, aged four, was almost as badly injured as his sister. He was wavering between consciousness and coma.

The roaring flames and crashing timbers forced the two rescuers out for the last time. It was clear the whole structure was about to collapse. This was the worst moment of all for Mike and Andrew. They could still hear groaning, and they knew that Frank Sitar, 20, and his brothers Walter, 11, and Bert, 10, were trapped inside, beyond anyone's help. The walls crashed in and the Sitar farmhouse became a funeral pyre for the three boys left inside. Their bodies were recovered later, when the charred ruins had cooled. Despite the selfless bravery of Mike and Andrew, six members of the Sitar family had perished in the fire, and the only survivor, little Paul, was near death.

It was soon obvious that there was a lot more going on in this case than just an accidental fire. As it turned out, all the victims had suffered terrible head injuries, which were clearly not caused by crashing debris. It looked to Mike, Andrew and the police like someone had attacked the family members with an axe and had then set the house on fire. Whoever had done this had also barred the front door from the outside to ensure that none of the Sitars would escape the blaze.

Someone had definitely murdered six people, and probably seven—it appeared that four-year-old Paul Sitar was unlikely to pull through. Manitoba Provincial Police (MPP) officers began to sift through the still-smouldering ashes, looking for any evidence they could find.

Then, amazingly, the police were given the information they were seeking, and it came from the lips of young Paul as he slipped in and out of consciousness a few hours after the fire. "Tom did it to us," he said.

Minutes after uttering these words, Paul was rushed on a special Canadian National train from Elma to Winnipeg, where an ambulance met the train and took him to St. Boniface Hospital.

Back in Elma, officers scoured what remained of the Sitar farmhouse to make sure that Thomas (Tom) Hreshkoski, Martin Sitar's nephew, hadn't died in the blaze. The 28-year-old Hreshkoski had been living with the Sitars and working on their farm as a labourer for over a year. Once authorities were certain that Hreshkoski's remains were not among the debris, they threw out a dragnet for him. It was the largest manhunt to be launched across the Manitoba prairie in years.

The man they were hunting was a Polish immigrant who had been living in Canada for several years, first in Sudbury, Ontario, and then in Winnipeg. While he lived in Sudbury,

Hreshkoski had been convicted of assault and served a six-month term in prison. But his time in Winnipeg had been much more peaceful—no one there seemed to realize he had any potential for violence. Nor was there any record of his exhibiting mental problems. He had lived in Winnipeg with two men, one of whom described him as "hardworking, and a man of great strength." And clearly, his uncle had had no inkling there was any problem. Martin Sitar had given him work and had found him to be a reliable worker who started his chores early each day.

The MPP thought Hreshkoski might have hopped a train to escape the area. If he had moved swiftly, he could have reached the nearby town of Whitemouth and boarded either a Canadian National or Canadian Pacific train, as both had pulled in there since the murder. But when railway staff were contacted, they assured police that no one fitting Hreshkoski's description had boarded either train. Next, MPP officers set up checkpoints on the road to Hadashville to the south and Lewis to the west.

Once they knew that Hreshkoski hadn't died in the fire or hopped a train, police began to wonder if he was trying to hide somewhere outdoors. As the blizzard that had blown in early that morning continued, they grew quite certain that he would soon face death from frostbite and exposure. Though Hreshkoski was a heavy-set man with considerable strength, even he would not survive long in such harsh conditions.

The next day, Saturday, shortly after 4 p.m., Paul Sitar died from his head injuries and burns. As the *Winnipeg Free Press* put it, the death toll of the "maniacal murderer who ran amok in the little household" now stood at seven.

Later that night, authorities thought they had Hreshkoski when a Polish stranger closely matching his description was seen sneaking off a freight train at Carroll, just south of Brandon and hundreds of kilometres west of Elma. The suspect was arrested farther south, in the town of Minto. He was then taken to the cells in Boissevain, where he gave police the marvellously unpronounceable name of Waswle Twerdosrid and claimed he'd never even been to Elma. Meanwhile, the MPP officers in Winnipeg, full of hope, raced to Boissevain. There they quickly established that Twerdosrid was exactly who he said he was. The search for Hreshkoski continued.

In the next three days, word of the huge manhunt spread throughout the southern Manitoba prairie, even as far as a tiny logging camp near the railway town of Contour, 16 kilometres west of Elma. This was lucky for the police. Five days after the massacre, Bob Lawry, a logger in the camp, had heard a strange wailing sound coming from the railway tracks nearby. When he went to investigate, he was shocked to find a heavy-set man with broad shoulders sitting on the ground and crying for food. The man appeared to be badly frostbitten. Lawry half-carried, half-dragged the starving man into the logging camp, where the stranger wolfed down the food offered him.

Suddenly, Lawry remembered the description of the wanted mass murderer. In a flash he realized he'd just captured the most wanted man in Canada. The loggers quickly got word of the capture to Whitemouth. Constable Percy Valder of the MPP instructed the loggers to get the fugitive on the train to Elma, and he'd meet them there. The suspect was far too weak to resist the loggers, and they delivered him to the constable, who promptly arrested him. In no time he was delivered to Winnipeg, where he was promptly locked up in the old provincial jail on Vaughan Street.

This time there was no mistake. This was Thomas Hreshkoski, and he was ready to confess. The words that came from his lips were almost unbelievable. Oh yes, he had slaughtered all seven members of his uncle's family with an axe. "The devil made me do it," he told them. Not just the devil. He'd also had evil spirits, ghosts and his own special demon instructing him to kill them.

The details that emerged from the confession were chilling. According to Hreshkoski, the day of the murders was like any other. He had risen early and started on his first chores, which included milking the cows. His Uncle Martin was up and busy as well. The two men carried on with their work until suddenly, Hreshkoski's special demon spoke inside his head. Hreshkoski went to the barn, fetched an axe and went into the farmhouse.

He killed his uncle first. Then he murdered everyone

else as they slept, going methodically from bedroom to bedroom until he was certain all seven family members were dead. Hreshkoski claimed he hadn't felt any animosity towards his uncle or the rest of the family. They'd treated him well, but he had to obey his demon. The last thing he did before the flames took hold of the house was to take all the bread he could find in the kitchen. And for five days, after building a small camp, he'd wandered around in the cold with only the bread and melted snow for sustenance.

When the police released details of the arrest and confession, the *Winnipeg Free Press* blasted the story across the front page of the February 3 newspaper, under the huge headline: 'GHOSTS' CAUSE OF ELMA CRIMES POLICE STATE FARM HAND ADMITS SLAYING FAMILY.

The next day, Hreshkoski, who by then had been formally charged with Martin Sitar's murder, was transferred to the provincial jail at Headingley to await examination by a leading psychiatrist. When police sifted through the burned ruins of the Sitar home, they had discovered a blackened axe head and thought they'd found the murder weapon. But Hreshkoski corrected them. No, he said, the axe he'd used was out in the countryside. He'd taken it with him to chop wood so that he could stay warm while he was hiding. He told them precisely where to find it. And they did, five kilometres from the Sitar house, exactly where he said it would be. Still heavily bloodstained, it was in his snow shelter along with a crosscut saw and an overcoat.

Hreshkoski then told an incredible story about the voices of his devils and ghosts. Over and over, he repeated one specific detail that no sane man would likely ever invent. He explained the final orders that had driven him to commit one of Manitoba's worst-ever massacres were given by his special little demon—his fly.

Hreshkoski's murder trial opened in March 1932 at the spring assizes. A reporter covering the trial for the *Winnipeg Free Press* wrote that the accused looked like "some hunted creature with wild staring eyes and a vacant look," adding that many people thought he was completely insane. Indeed, it was pretty widely felt that he'd be found not guilty because of his obvious psychosis.

Jury members heard that on the day he was arrested Hreshkoski didn't wait to reach Winnipeg before confessing. He first blurted out everything to Constable Percy Valder, the Whitemouth MPP officer who'd fetched him from the loggers. Valder told the jury he was the first to hear the chilling story, adding that Hreshkoski had told him, "The devil was in my heart before Christmas. The devil told me to kill Martin Sitar and all his family, and then go away and hide in the bushes."

Even the prosecution's psychiatrist, Dr. A.T. Mathers, reckoned Hreshkoski hadn't been in his right mind when he'd wielded his axe. In various interviews, Hreshkoski had told the doctor that he suffered hallucinations. He had been visited by the devil, complete with horns on his head and a tail. Several times on different days, the devil had told him to kill the family. His special little demon had told him the same thing as well.

The jury then heard more amazing testimony from Nick Darowec, a jailbird who shared a cell with the accused. Hreshkoski had told Darowec all about his demon fly. Prior to this conversation, Darowec had already thought that Hreshkoski was odd. After it, he was sure that Hreshkoski was not just odd, but crazy.

The psychiatrist for the prosecution confirmed for the jury that Hreshkoski believed he had a special demon in the form of a large, buzzing black fly. Later, a guard testified that Hreshkoski had tried to commit suicide in his cell two days before one of his court hearings.

All the facts were before the jury, and an insanity verdict was expected right away. But after five hours the jury returned to the courtroom unable to come up with a unanimous decision. The judge sent them away for the night. By the following morning, they had resolved their differences. To many people's surprise, the jury members dismissed all talk of insanity. They found Thomas Hreshkoski guilty of murder. Justice Adamson pronounced the death sentence and set June 7, 1932, as the date for his execution.

Oddly, Hreshkoski never once claimed insanity as a defence. Yes, he was quick to confess to everyone he met that he had killed the whole Sitar family because his devils had told him to do it. But the devils were his sole motive. Before he went to trial, psychiatric tests had been carried out on him at Winnipeg General Hospital. The MPP later quoted the psychiatrist, saying that the doctor had backed Hreshkoski's claims that he wasn't insane. Clearly, the jury listened to the professional.

If Hreshkoski were tried in today's legal system, a good defence lawyer would most certainly argue insanity on his behalf. If that failed, the lawyer would appeal Hreshkoski's death sentence to every higher court available. No lawyer today would leave Hreshkoski hanging on the whim of a possible last-minute reprieve from Ottawa. However, it was 1932, and no appeal was lodged on Hreshkoski's behalf.

On June 7, 1932, Hreshkoski was preparing to undergo his punishment when an unexpected communication arrived from the Department of Justice. At the very last moment, Thomas Hreshkoski's death sentence was commuted. He was taken away to Stony Mountain Penitentiary to spend the rest of his life in jail.

Could it be that someone in Ottawa realized there must have been some element of insanity in Hreshkoski's actions? After all, many other killers have been found insane after blaming voices in their heads for prompting their murderous attacks. But Hreshkoski, initially at least, convinced the entire legal system that his demon fly had made him do it.

CHAPTER

5

Hitler's Legacy

IF EVER THE PUNISHMENT FIT the crime, this was it: an eye for an eye, a tooth for a tooth and a neck for a neck. Two victims were hanged by a lynch mob; five of the murderers were hanged by the law, four on the same day. It was the largest legal mass hanging in Canada in the 20th century. And that was only the tip of the iceberg.

This amazing murder story had, under the surface, elements never seen before anywhere in Canada. The two victims—one beaten up and hanged in 1943 and the other suffering an identical death in 1944—were German prisoners of war (POWs) in Internment Camp 132 at Medicine Hat, Alberta. And their merciless killers, five of whom ended their days swinging at the end of a rope off a prison gallows in

Lethbridge, were all fellow prisoners. They were Nazi Gestapo men who ran a regime of brutality and terror among their fellow Germans inside the POW camp.

Faced with this incredible problem, who would be tasked to sort it all out? The men were all German military personnel in a prisoner-of-war environment. Should they be court-martialled by the German military? Or by the Canadian military? In Germany? Or in Canada? Or even in Britain? Eventually, it fell to none of these. It fell to the RCMP, who treated the two cases as straightforward murders committed on Canadian soil. The trials were processed through Alberta's criminal justice system, with civilian prison nooses tightening round the necks of the guilty.

By the time the Allies won the battle of North Africa in May 1943, they had taken hundreds of thousands of prisoners. Canada played a major role in the logistical nightmare of dealing with this mass of prisoners. Five of the largest German POW camps were built in Alberta, at Medicine Hat, Lethbridge, Kananaskis, Ozada and Wainwright. By 1943 more than 12,000 Germans were being housed in Medicine Hat Internment Camp 132. Dealing with such huge numbers of prisoners made it impossible for the Canadian authorities to closely control everything happening inside the camp. This allowed the forceful Nazi element among the Germans to develop a powerful Gestapo presence. The prisoners who were Nazis saw it as their duty to use bully-boy violence and intimidation to instill their extreme pro-Hitler doctrine in their fellow Germans.

Two categories of German prisoners were especially despised by the Gestapo leadership in the camp. One consisted of former members of the French Foreign Legion, whom the leadership considered to have been a major weakness in the German war effort in North Africa. The leaders believed the Legionnaires had been the cause of Germany losing that continent. The other category were those considered traitors to Hitler, especially Communists.

Among the ranks of the former French Foreign Legionnaires in the camp was August Plaszek, who had been a farmer as a young man. He served in Africa after the First World War. In the 1930s he returned to Germany, left the Legionnaires when the Nazis were coming into power, and joined the German army. He was sent to North Africa, where he fought in the 361st Afrika Regiment, a unit consisting entirely of former Legionnaires. Plaszek was captured by the Allies on December 12, 1941, and shipped as a POW to Canada, ending up as prisoner number ME04024 in Internment Camp 132. The Gestapo terror squads soon targeted the 40-year-old prisoner as one of the despised ex-Legionnaire outcasts. Many Germans in the camp believed that anyone who'd joined the French Foreign Legion must have had a criminal background and that those among the Legionnaire ranks were perverts and outcasts from society.

On June 22, 1943, Plaszek was found hanged from a

beam in the west recreation drill hall of the camp. He had been beaten bloody and smashed in the head with a stone before being strung up. Word was the Gestapo leadership claimed to have chalked up two strikes against the ex-Legionnaires. First, they said, they'd uncovered a plot by a group of the despised prisoners to overthrow their control of the camp. Second, they claimed the hated men had tried to negotiate their way out of the camp so they could join the Free French forces in the war again—against Germany.

They rounded up four Legionnaires, intending to interrogate them in a kangaroo court one after the other. They found the first man, Christian Schulz, guilty. But before Gestapo punishment could be meted out to him, he had the presence of mind to make a bolt for it. He ran towards the Canadian prison guards, pursued by hundreds of prisoners intent on stopping him from escaping his due retribution. Several guards helped him over the interior barbed wire and into their safekeeping, firing a warning shot into the air to keep the crowd at bay. Now the mob, incensed at losing their prey, herded back to where the next three men were awaiting interrogation. They seized on Plaszek, who hadn't even been questioned yet, and dragged him outside where someone smashed him over the head with a large stone. Then he was beaten, dragged inside the recreation drill hall and hanged.

There was no point in the camp's murder squad killing an enemy they considered a traitor to the Nazi cause unless the slaying was carried out in public. It had to be in full view of other German POWs to maximize their message of terror. Many prisoners witnessed the defenceless Plaszek being dragged into the hall by the Gestapo mob and hanged. The witnesses knew better than to talk about what they'd seen with anyone from outside the camp. After all, they had to survive day after day, possibly for years, locked in the camp with the paranoid Gestapo killers who — ran the place. Imagine the difficulty faced by the RCMP when they tried to persuade witnesses to reveal what they'd seen, let alone convincing them to stand up in court and testify against the camp's Gestapo.

Within 24 hours of Plaszek's body being cut down and taken into Medicine Hat for autopsy, RCMP corporal Arthur "Johnny" Bull, a Criminal Investigation Department (CID) detective, arrived at the camp and was taken straight to the crime scene in the drill hall. His next stop was the Pattison Funeral Home in Medicine Hat, where he examined Plaszek's badly battered body. So ended the first day of an investigation that would take years to reach the courts. Corporal Bull was soon travelling to other POW camps across Canada where some of his potential witnesses had been transferred. This was to become the most frustrating and time-consuming investigation of his career.

If the fall of the German armies in North Africa had played an obscure role in the hanging murder of August Plaszek in a far distant POW camp on the prairies of Canada, another major moment in the war led to a second hanging murder in the same camp. This connection was far more obscure and seized on by the camp's Gestapo with even greater relish. This time they were acting on words from the Führer, Adolf Hitler himself, or so they said.

It was September 11, 1944, when German POW Dr. Karl Lehmann, 38, a well-educated professor of languages who was fluent in English, French and Russian, was found hanged from a pipe in the ceiling of Barracks D6. Lehmann was an Afrika Corps veteran corporal who had fought at the battle of Stalingrad. Like Plaszek, he had been beaten before being strung up. Once again, there were witnesses among the German prisoners who watched the camp's Gestapo death squad take a helpless victim from among their ranks and apply their inevitable justice. As before, these were not witnesses who were going to offer testimony voluntarily. None of them wanted to put his head in the Gestapo noose.

Word running through the camp this time was that the Gestapo leadership had Lehmann near the top of their death list for five reasons. The professor, who'd taught at the University of Erlangen in Germany, was better educated than the Gestapo leaders. He had strong anti-Nazi views, and some said he'd been a reporter for a Communist newspaper in Germany. He was, apparently, quick to spread his Communist doctrine to other German POWs. In addition, they claimed he was an informant, ratting on the Gestapo leadership in the camp to the Canadian authorities.

Above all, he wasn't afraid to tell anyone who'd listen that Germany would lose the war.

Adding to Lehmann's slim chances of survival were the explicit words of the Führer. On July 20, 1944, back in Germany, one of Hitler's senior military officers, Colonel Graf von Stauffenberg, was about to attend a meeting at Hitler's heavily defended headquarters in Rastenburg. The colonel was the spearhead of a highly organized team of senior German officers who were sure the Führer was leading Germany to annihilation, and who were planning his assassination. As the meeting began in the map room where the Führer plotted out the conquest of the world, Stauffenberg put his suitcase down under the table, as close to Hitler as he could wedge it. Then, suddenly called to deal with an urgent telephone call from Berlin, Stauffenberg left the room and never looked back—not even when an enormous explosion ripped through the room, his suitcase bomb having exploded exactly on time. Pleased they had obviously rid the world of this hated megalomaniac, Stauffenberg and his fellow conspirators began plans to set up their alternative government, which would run Germany now Hitler was gone. Except—a few minutes after the blast—Hitler miraculously stumbled out of the debris of the shattered building. Four of his senior officers were dead, others were critically injured, but he suffered only minor injuries. In a bizarre twist of fate, a sturdy wooden table support between him and the bomb had saved his life.

Hitler, in a speech hours later, vented his fury against the conspirators, and vowed that this "gang of criminal elements," this "gang of ambitious and miserable creatures" would be "ruthlessly exterminated." Hitler gave general orders that any good German soldier finding a traitor anywhere should kill him instantly. He gave instructions to the hangman who was ordered to execute the conspirators, "I want them to be hanged—hung up like carcasses of meat."

Several POWs in Medicine Hat had secret radios on which they could pick up transmissions from Germany. And the words—straight from Hitler's mouth—were taken literally by the Gestapo fanatics in the camp. They undoubtedly had a traitor in their midst: Dr. Karl Lehmann with his Communist teachings and his predictions that the Fatherland was about to be destroyed by the Allies. But time was running short. The POW Gestapo leaders knew that the hard-core Nazis in the camp were being shipped out to a different camp the next day. So if Hitler's words were to be obeyed and this traitor was to be hanged, it would have to be that night. And it was. The murder squad was assembled in a hut classroom, and Lehmann was summoned. He went in and never came out. He was later found hung like a carcass of meat from a pipe near the ceiling.

RCMP corporal Johnny Bull was soon calling his senior officers back to the camp for the new murder. At least with the Plaszek murder, Bull knew the killers were already physically in custody inside the Medicine Hat

POW camp. All he had to do was find out which of the 12,500 POWs they were! But now, immediately after the Lehmann hanging, his potential suspects were being farmed out to other POW camps across Canada. Although this set of killers was also in custody, Bull would have to work to find out not only who they were, but also in which camp they were being held.

This time, the influence played by the Second World War on the drama inside the Medicine Hat camp worked to Bull's advantage. When the war ended and Germany was smashed, the threat from the Nazis inside the POW camps diminished. The German prisoners, who had been too terrified to reveal what they knew, now began talking and even began naming names. Most of those said to have been involved in the Plaszek murder had been shipped some time ago either to the Neys POW camp in Ontario or to the Lethbridge POW camp in Alberta, which was where the RCMP carried out extensive interviews. On October 10, 1945, more than two years after Plaszek was killed, three men were arrested. And on November 16, they were formally charged with his murder.

When the first of the three trials started in 1946, the *Medicine Hat Daily News* identified the three prisoners, now formally in custody, and told something about their backgrounds. Sergeant Werner Schwalb, 30, who was born during the First World War, was a baker and a cook. He joined the German army shortly before the Second World

War and won the Iron Cross, First Class, as a Panzer tank gunner when the rampaging Germans were sweeping across France in 1940. On January 17, 1942, while serving as an infantryman in Egypt, he was captured by South African troops who were fighting for the Allies. Four months later, he was one of thousands of POWs shipped to Canada on the HMS *Queen Elizabeth*. Schwalb eventually ended up as prisoner number ME038848 in the Medicine Hat internment camp.

The other two accused men were Adolf Kratz, 24, from Koblenz in Germany and Lance Corporal Johannes Wittinger, 30, from Graz in Austria. They were both captured on the same day—May 29, 1942—in Tobruk by the Free French forces as the battle for North Africa raged. Kratz had been a carpenter before the war. After joining the German army, he served in France, then the Russian front and Italy, before being sent to North Africa, where he was captured. Wittinger, a truck driver, also served in Italy before being sent to North Africa, where he was wounded and received the Iron Cross. He was captured only 10 days after he arrived.

Schwalb was the first to stand trial in the Medicine Hat courthouse, his case opening on February 25, 1946. Witnesses first described how they had seen one prisoner running for the wire and escaping from a mob of prisoners to the safety of Canadian guards. Next they described seeing a second prisoner being dragged into the recreation room where he was found hanged. Then Crown Prosecutor Walter Donald Gow, KC, introduced evidence to prove one of the killers was Schwalb. The judge allowed some prisoners to remain anony- ⌐ mous to save them from possible reprisals back in Germany. One testified that Schwalb came into his room in the camp after the murder, his hands covered in blood, and uttered what turned out to be some very prophetic words: "This walk can lead to a hanging for me. We hanged one there. Should they hang me, I will die as a German soldier."

Another anonymous POW, a Luftwaffe pilot, pointed out Schwalb as one of those who hanged Plaszek. Yet another POW testified that he went into the recreation hall moments after the killing, saw Plaszek's body hanging, and saw Schwalb standing in the hall with blood on his hands.

To combat the seemingly damning evidence pointing straight at Schwalb, his defence lawyer, L.S. Turcotte of Lethbridge, submitted that the real murderers weren't those in the recreation hall that night, but instead were the ⌐ three Nazi Gestapo camp leaders who had incited the men to take action. The jury didn't buy that, and on March 13, 1946, they came back after deliberating for just over an hour with a verdict: guilty of murder. Chief Justice W.R. Howson sentenced Schwalb to be hanged on June 26.

Adolph Kratz came to trial next, when a different jury heard the same general description of the killing, followed by testimony proving that Kratz was another of the killers. One witness told the jury Kratz spoke to him twice, once going into the recreation room and again as he left the building. On the way in, Kratz said he was going to take part in hanging a prisoner. On the way out he said, "Now we have hanged one of those swine," and bragged how they had wound the rope around the prisoner's neck. Another witness said Kratz told him it was his duty to kill the traitors.

Defence lawyer Turcotte, faced with the same damning evidence against Kratz that he faced against Schwalb, tried to deflect the blame again onto the Nazi Gestapo leadership. It failed again, although this time it took the jury a few more hours to reach a guilty verdict. Kratz was sentenced to hang on the same day as Schwalb.

As soon as Kratz was sentenced, a new jury was sworn in and the trial of Wittinger began. Defence lawyer Turcotte had more ammunition to work with this time. He pointed out that the Crown hadn't found a single witness who picked out Wittinger as being among the killers. And astoundingly, Sergeant Werner Schwalb, the already-condemned prisoner awaiting the hangman's noose, testified that he didn't see Wittinger at the recreation hall that night, nor that whole day. This time, after deliberating for more than two hours, the jury returned a verdict of not guilty, and Wittinger was later sent home to Austria.

Less than 48 hours before the death sentences were to be carried out for the two who were found guilty, a telegram was delivered from the governor general saying that he had taken note of the plea for mercy submitted by the jury that had found Kratz guilty. He then commuted Kratz's sentence to life imprisonment. No such telegram came for Schwalb, though. On June 26, 1946, they walked him to the gallows. His final words as they placed the black hood over his head were, "My Führer, I follow thee." His prophecy of being hanged and dying as a soldier came true.

While these three Plaszek trials were under way in Medicine Hat, Corporal Bull and other RCMP detectives were still chasing down suspects in the Lehmann murder in various POW camps across Canada. On April 6, 1946, they arrested four German POW suspects and charged them with the murder. Three of these four were bomber pilots in the Luftwaffe, whose planes had gone down over Britain. The fourth was a soldier. They were Sergeant Major Bruno Perzonowsky, Sergeant Willi Mueller, Sergeant Major Heinrich Busch and Sergeant Walter Wolf.

Perzonowsky, 34, from East Prussia, joined the Luftwaffe before the war and had flown 60 operational bombing raids over Britain. He won the Iron Cross, First Class, before his plane was shot down and crashed in the Welsh mountains on April 14, 1941. The career of Mueller, 31, began in the German Navy, but he transferred to the Luftwaffe and had flown 87 bombing raids over Britain before a Spitfire shot his aircraft down in Scotland on May 6, 1941. Mueller broke both his legs and his back in the crash. Busch, 29, was less experienced, having flown 26 bombing raids before he flew his aircraft into a barrage balloon cable over Norfolk, England, on February 18, 1941, and was brought down. Wolf, a 29-year-old soldier in Rommel's Afrika Corps, was a former tax inspector. He had served in the German invasion of France in 1940 and was later sent to fight with Rommel's army in North Africa, where he earned the Iron Cross, Second Class, before being captured on January 17, 1942.

On June 24, 1946, the day word reached the Lethbridge jail that Kratz's death sentence had been commuted to life imprisonment, Perzonowsky's trial opened in Medicine Hat. This time the prosecution had the added strength of a confession from the accused man. Perzonowsky repeated to the court that he had given the order to have Lehmann removed. Perzonowsky was, therefore, perceived as the ringleader. His defence lawyer, George Rice, KC, faced with his client's statement of guilt, worked hard to persuade the judge that the trial was being heard in the wrong place. He submitted that Perzonowsky's actions as a military man in time of war were an act of war, not a crime, and that he should be subject to a military court martial, not a civilian trial. Further, he argued that the trial should be held in Germany, not Canada. Rice's argument failed, and the jury took just 60 minutes to find Perzonowsky guilty of murder. Chief Justice Howson sentenced Perzonowsky to be hanged in the Lethbridge jail on October 16, 1946.

In his book *Behind Canadian Barbed Wire*, David J. Carter talks about George Krause, one of the RCMP officers who was at the sentencing. Years later Krause recalled that just as the judge pronounced the dreaded words, "You shall be taken to the place of execution and there be hanged by the neck until dead. May the Lord have mercy on your soul," the nearby school bell started to toll. Krause told Carter that every face in the courtroom turned white. He described it as one of the most gripping moments of his life.

When Wolf came to trial, several witnesses identified him as having been personally involved in hanging the prisoner Lehmann. Even Willi Mueller, his co-accused, gave evidence for the Crown. Wolf himself later admitted his part in the crime, but justified his actions by saying he had been ordered to take part by Perzonowsky. Once again, defence lawyer Rice tried to have the entire hearing declared null and void. Once again he failed. After nearly three hours of deliberations, the jury found Wolf guilty of murder and he too was sentenced to be hanged in the Lethbridge jail.

When Busch came to trial, the jury had an easier task. His own statements spelled out the role he had played in the murder: how he had hurriedly tried to wash Lehmann's blood off his clothing, and how he couldn't sleep that night because he knew he had helped murder a man. One witness testified that it was Busch who tied the rope to the pipe under the ceiling from which Lehmann was hanged. The jury found him guilty of murder, and he was sentenced to be hanged with the others.

The fourth and final trial, that of Willi Mueller, was the most open-and-shut case of the four. Mueller had made a sworn statement detailing his role in the murder. He was clearly expecting to receive leniency in return for the crucial evidence he had given for the Crown, which had helped the prosecution secure the convictions of his co-accused. But it didn't work. The jury soon found him guilty, and he became the fourth man sentenced to be hanged for the murder. All were to die on October 16, 1946, but legal delays put the date back to December 18.

In the final hours before their executions, three of the men—Perzonowsky, Wolf and Busch—tried to cheat the gallows by committing suicide. Apparently they had learned they were to be hanged alongside a Calgary pedophile sex-killer, which they considered too degrading to contemplate. Someone smuggled razor blades, hidden inside a book, to them. But the guards were keeping a close watch on the condemned men and saw what happened. They reached them in their blood-splashed cells in time to save them for the hangman. It is thought that Mueller did not make the attempt to kill himself because he was hoping that his actions in turning on his fellow Germans during the trials might still earn him a last-minute reprieve. It didn't. All four were hanged two-by-two, with Perzonowsky and Busch going first, immediately followed by Mueller and Wolf. And right after that the Calgary pedophile sex-killer was executed.

After the hangings, all seven of the hanged German POWs—the two victims and their five murderers—were buried under the exercise yard at Lethbridge Provincial Jail. Authorities reckoned they were safe from desecration there. At first no one claimed the bodies, but more than 20 years later, in 1970, the German War Graves Commission requested they be exhumed. The Commission was moving the remains of all German POWs to a central cemetery in Kitchener, Ontario, which has such a rich German heritage that it used to be called Berlin. When the remains were reburied, the authorities kept the German killers together, pairing some of them in the same graves. Schwalb, who killed Plaszek, and Perzonowsky, ringleader of the Lehmann killers, were buried together. Busch and Mueller, two of the Luftwaffe pilots turned murderers, shared another grave. Wolf, the Afrika Corps soldier, was buried nearby. Fittingly, the remains of their two victims, Plaszek and Lehmann, were buried elsewhere in the cemetery with German military personnel—well away from the killers.

6

The Kleenex
in the Courtroom

EVERYONE EXPERIENCES THAT INEVITABLE URGE: your head is blocked, you feel a cold drip on the tip of your nostril, and you just have to blow your nose. You grab a Kleenex, use it and throw it in the garbage. It is the most trivial, unremarkable moment of your whole day. Ryan Jason Love did exactly that. It was the biggest mistake of his life. It cost him 20 years behind bars—and it played a role in changing criminal law across Canada.

Love's dripping nose afflicted him in a motel room in Gibsons, on the Sunshine Coast of British Columbia, in the summer of 1992. What made it all so vital had begun on a dark and deserted street 1,400 kilometres away in Banff, Alberta, more than two years earlier.

The Kleenex in the Courtroom

In the early hours of May 17, 1990, Banff cabbie Lucie Turmel, 23, is parked on the street. Her fiancé, Jeff Hayes, is talking with her at her car window. At 1:30 a.m. she gets a call from the Taxi-Taxi & Tours dispatcher, Bruce Feriancek. She waves to Jeff as she drives off to The Works, a nightclub at the Banff Springs Hotel, where she picks up the three waiting fares—a man and two women.

Feriancek expects that he'll hear from her on the radio after a while, but he doesn't. The silence is unnerving. Feriancek feels uneasy. Meanwhile, not far away on Squirrel Street, security guard Cindy Smith makes a shocking discovery. It's 1:45 a.m. and a woman's body is lying on the street in a spreading pool of blood. Police soon cordon off the area. For Banff RCMP constable Nigel Paterson, the crime scene is a short walk, less than a block from his home. He's there in seconds with the other officers. They immediately establish that the victim is dead. Cabbie Lucie Turmel's life lasted only the shortest moment after her killer savagely stabbed her in the middle of the road and drove off in her cab.

Just a few moments later, fellow cabbie Larry Laundreau sees Turmel's cab being driven through the darkened streets with a man behind the wheel. He swings his cab in behind the obviously stolen taxi, but the killer sees immediately he's being tailed and hits the gas pedal. They touch speeds up to 100 kilometres per hour as the killer tries to give Laundreau the slip. When he reaches the section of Banff just south of the bridge over the river, he dumps the taxi and flees into thick bushes and trees. Laundreau gives chase but loses him. The killer obviously knows his way around Banff. He disappears into the night.

* * *

The townsfolk of Banff, the internationally known jewel of the Rocky Mountains, were stunned. The slaying of a vulnerable young woman late at night was the first murder in their midst that anyone could remember. The town's population was already swollen by thousands of spring tourists, and the flood of visitors had just begun. Now there was a killer on the loose—one who was perfectly capable of inflicting a savage and murderous attack on a helpless woman for just a few bucks. The RCMP revealed that Lucie had been repeatedly stabbed in a frenzy of blows for not much more than $100, her evening's take.

Lucie originally came from Lévis, Quebec, where her parents, Jean and Denise, still lived. Their daughter first worked at the Grizzly House Restaurant in Banff, where she met her fiancé, before deciding to drive a taxi cab for a living.

At first, the RCMP had little to go on. They had the description of the fleeing man who had been chased by Laundreau, and they had found the murder weapon, a huge hunting knife, which they photographed and publicized in the hope that someone would recognize it.

Then on June 3, nearly three weeks after the murder, they had their first big break. Tests carried out by crime

Glimmer of hope helps family to cope

He's a man living in hope.

The father of slain Banff cabbie, Lucie Turmel, may live 4,000 km away in Levis, Que., but her memory is close to his heart.

For the first time, he speaks out about his daughter's death.

And every month for the past year — since his daughter was brutally stabbed to death — Jean Turmel has received a phone call.

Banff RCMP Cpl. Bryan Gerrie, who leads the hunt for Lucie's killer, updates him.

With each call, Jean's hopes rise that they're nearer to catching the killer.

But he still hasn't received any good news.

The murder of his 24-year-old daughter is unsolved, despite a massive investigation that's spread as far afield as Japan.

Now Jean, 62, is hoping renewed publicity on the one-year anniversary of the killing brings a new lead.

"We still remember the policeman coming to the house and telling my wife Lucie had been murdered. I was at my office," said Jean.

"The police here said they had received a telegram from Banff. They told my colleague here that my girl had been killed in Banff.

"It is a terrible thing for the whole family."

This week, Jean, his wife Denise, Lucie's two elder brothers and the rest of the family will be holding a mass in her memory.

One person at the mass will be the father of Lucie's fiance, Jeff Hayes.

Hayes, 30, an employee of the Grizzly House restaurant in Banff, and Lucie met when she, too, was employed at the restaurant.

Sadly, Hayes met Lucie's family for the first time at her funeral in Quebec.

This week, Hayes is away on vacation and won't be in Banff on the anniversary of his fiancee's slaying.

Friends say he was shattered, and has spent the year trying his best to put Lucie's death behind him.

The people closest to Lucie aren't confident that her killer will be caught after a year.

But her family in Quebec are at least pleased that a renewed effort is being made.

Whatever the outcome of the fresh publicity, however, the coming week will be a terrible time for Lucie's family.

"This is a bad memory for us. This week in May will always be a bad memory for us," said Jean.

A killer is on the loose. Can you help catch him? A year ago this week — May 17 — Banff cabbie Lucie Turmel, 24, was stabbed to death and left in a pool of blood on a Banff street. RCMP are appealing through the Crime Stoppers' program for public help in trying to capture the killer. Sun reporter Peter Smith now takes you through the background to the Lucie Turmel killing. Maybe it'll help to jog your memory — and help to find this killer.

Lucie Turmel's wallet, top, and coat, bottom, were stolen by her murderer. Police believe the knife above was used to kill her. The Banff cabbie, left, was killed last May 17.

Murder leaves legacy of suspicion

No Banff cabbie will ever forget the night Lucie Turmel was murdered.

It just as easily could have been any one of them.

Bruce Feriancek was one of three cabbies from Taxi Taxi — the company which Turmel drove for — working that night.

"I still go to bed some nights and think, what if it was different. It could have been me," he said.

Feriancek, like every other Banff cabbie, knows the murder was a robbery that went tragically wrong.

"It could have been . . . any cab in Banff," he said.

Turmel, a native of Quebec, had worked for two years in Banff in restaurants, with other taxi firms, before joining Taxi Taxi.

On May 17, her fifth night, she picked up three customers at The Works nightclub in the Banff Springs Hotel at 1:30 a.m.

Police have never found these three people.

Nearly 30 minutes later, Turmel's body was found stabbed on Squirrel St. Her cash, wallet and jacket were missing.

It's thought she was killed for as little as $100.

Shortly afterwards, a Taxi Taxi colleague saw Turmel's cab being driven by a man, and gave chase. Feriancek remembers being on the road behind the two cabs. The mystery man abandoned Turmel's cab, and fled into the bush, and has never been found.

A knife police say was the murder weapon was found nearby.

Feriancek thinks police made one mistake.

"The man could never have got back into town without crossing the bridge over the Bow River. They should have closed the bridge that night. Then they would have had him," he said.

The murder hunt was hampered by the problem of tracing thousands of visitors.

The killer may have been a tourist. Some visitor may have seen something vital without realizing it.

First, the RCMP took details of 3,000 visitors in town that night. They then wrote to every one — across the States, and as far abroad as Japan.

So far, the vital lead has not come in.

Investigators interviewed 1,500 people in Banff in the first few weeks of the inquiry. But even more than $7,000 in reward money offered by Taxi Taxi owner Tim Powell hasn't brought a breakthrough.

Lucie Turmel's death has brought one lasting legacy to the cabbies of Banff. They are much more suspicious now than they ever were before her slaying.

"We're very careful now about who we pick up," said Feriancek. If anyone gives even the first hint of trouble, they're out of the cab.

"That's one thing Lucie left us. We're very wary now."

A page from the *Calgary Sun*, May 12, 1991

laboratory technicians revealed that Lucie wasn't the only one who had shed blood in the cab. The killer had been cut too and had left his own blood splashed inside the vehicle. The police appealed to the public to come forward if they knew of anyone who'd recently suffered unusual cuts.

But despite this lead and a reward of $12,000, the hunt for the murderer stalled. Even though inquiries spanned the globe, the slaying remained unsolved. At one stage, the search switched to Japan and the United States. Nearly 3,000 visitors to Banff who'd been in town on the night of the murder received letters asking for information. No credible leads turned up. One man on the RCMP's suspect list was traced to Paris, France. Investigators discovered he'd been murdered there, and they waited for a sample of his blood to arrive in Canada. The results eliminated him as a suspect.

Two years later, Banff's taxi-driver killing appeared on the television series *Unsolved Mysteries*, which gave the impression that the RCMP were so stumped they'd resorted to this last desperate measure for help. This wasn't strictly true. For many months, without revealing any clues to the public, they'd had two very strong suspects in their sights. The primary suspect was a man who had first hidden behind the perfect alibi—that he was already locked up in prison— until investigators discovered he was out on a day pass at the time of the slaying. What's more, he'd bragged about being the killer.

That wasn't enough to arrest him. The Mounties needed

much more, and they had a way of getting it. The ace up their sleeve was the knowledge that the killer had cut himself during his frenzied attack. The RCMP had recovered his blood from inside Lucie Turmel's cab, which meant they had the killer's DNA. This was a comparatively new weapon in the armoury of forensic scientists. In the early 1990s, DNA evidence had already been used in a few murder cases in Canada. The experts had assured the RCMP that if they ever had a prime suspect and could produce a sample of his DNA, they could use this science to eliminate him or nail him as the killer. Nearly 200 suspects had already volunteered their blood samples and been cleared by DNA comparison. But not this man, the prime suspect. He exercised his legal right not to give any bodily sample for DNA examination.

The second of their two main suspects exercised the same right and refused to give a blood sample. Among the 2,000 tips the RCMP had followed up was the name of a man who'd owned a large hunting knife exactly like the one featured in the press releases—the one forensic scientists had proved was the murder weapon. Investigators had found him and had questioned him about the knife, which he readily admitted was his. He'd bought it in Mexico, he said, but had left it behind in Banff when he left town. The suspect claimed he had nothing to do with the murder.

In spite of the fact that this man had owned the murder weapon at some time, was in Banff on the night of the murder and resembled the description of the killer, there was not enough evidence to arrest him. Investigators needed bodily samples from these two men—hair, blood, semen. But neither man was giving up anything.

RCMP undercover agents hatched a cunning plan. They tricked their primary suspect and in February 1992 got some of his hair without him having a clue who they were. In a flash it was on its way to the RCMP's DNA genetic testing laboratory in Ottawa. Nearly as quickly, the results came back. Negative. "He was eliminated. End of story," said Constable Paterson, who had doggedly stuck with the case since the night he was among the first to see Turmel's body on Squirrel Street.

With the prime suspect gone, the next in line—the knife man—rose to the top of the list. The inventive and cunning RCMP undercover agents went back to work again. This time their attempts to get the needed DNA samples from their suspect became even more devious. They got their suspect drunk at a boozy party and plucked some hairs from his head, joking about changing his hairstyle. It was a start, but they knew it might not be enough. So, by acting out roles as low-life criminals, they wheedled their way into his friendship. After several weeks, he began to trust them.

On July 16, 1992, they set their trap. They planned a meeting in a hotel room in Victoria, British Columbia. Their ploy was to discuss some criminal enterprise, as three petty villains might well do. At some stage during the evening, the two "low-life criminals" suggested going out to a cabaret, ostensibly to see if they could pick up some women. It was a good night. The drinks flowed, and they hit it off with three easy women who were happy to go back to the hotel room. They even brought pornographic movies with them. The suspect was in the trap. After a while, his two "buddies" and the women, who also happened to be undercover RCMP officers, left him alone. They waited, ready to recover the semen specimen they were sure he'd produce. But he didn't. Their meticulously laid plan failed. They were thwarted.

Undeterred, the persistent undercover cops stuck with it and a month later were passing the time at a motel in Gibsons with their suspect. Suddenly, out of the blue, the suspect felt that cold dribble in his nostril, blew his nose and threw the mucus-laden tissue in the garbage—right in front of them! Ryan Jason Love, never guessing what he had done, had just presented the cops with a perfect DNA sample. A sample that was voluntarily supplied. It would be completely acceptable in court as evidence against him—if it was relevant. Relevant? It was damning. The forensic scientists were as good as their promise. They matched the DNA samples and sent word to the RCMP. The blood in Lucie Turmel's cab had come from Ryan Love.

The RCMP knew exactly where to find him—on the southern end of Vancouver Island in Duncan, British Columbia, where he was a college student. At 5:30 p.m. on Thursday, November 12, 1992, Ryan Jason Love was arrested.

Striding purposefully behind him as he was marched across the tarmac at Calgary International Airport after his flight from British Columbia was Banff RCMP constable Paterson, the detective who'd dogged the killer at every turn.

Love's trial before Court of Queen's Bench justice Robert Cairns opened in Calgary on March 28, 1994, with a graphic description of the diminutive Lucie Turmel fighting for her life as her killer wielded his treacherous hunting knife. The struggle went on first inside her cab, then out on the deserted Banff street. Pathologist Dr. Ronald Roy said she'd suffered 35 injuries—17 stab wounds and 18 incisions—and 5 more defensive slices across her hands when she'd fought to grab the knife. One final blow severed the carotid artery in her neck, and she bled to death.

Then into the witness box stepped RCMP crime laboratory scientist Gary Verret, around whom the case would revolve. He told the judge his DNA testing had proved the blood found on the knife that Love admitted to owning was Lucie Turmel's blood, and that three bloodstains found inside her cab after the murder contained the same DNA found in a nasal mucus sample obtained from Love. And because Love's DNA was of an extremely rare type, the chances of the blood in the cab coming from someone other than Love were less than one in 230 billion. Another DNA expert, the top man in his field from Texas, testified that Gary Verret was being "ultra conservative." The odds were really more like 1.19 trillion to one.

Defence lawyer David Younggren's only real chance to weaken the damning evidence had already failed. He had tried to exclude the DNA evidence from being heard at all by arguing that the undercover tricks used by the RCMP to get their samples of Love's DNA (pulling his hair out and taking his discarded tissue without a warrant) were illegal. Justice Cairns disagreed, and the crucial DNA evidence was in.

On Wednesday, June 16, 1994, the judge found Love, then 22, guilty of second-degree murder. Two days later, after Assistant Chief Crown Attorney Harold Hagglund had described the killing as "a case of unmitigated evil," he handed down to Ryan Jason Love the mandatory life sentence, stipulating he have no chance of parole for 20 years, double the normal ineligibility period.

In sentencing Love, Justice Cairns said the most vital aspect of the whole case was the tough but futile fight for life Turmel had put up, during which the killer was cut with his own knife. This provided the evidence that ultimately convicted him, the blood that matched the DNA on that vital piece of tissue. This soiled Kleenex had put a murderer behind bars for the rest of his life—but even more amazing was what followed.

Love's lawyer, thwarted in his first attempt to get the DNA evidence excluded from the trial, quickly launched an appeal against the conviction on the grounds that the RCMP had breached Love's Charter rights. After all, Younggren claimed, the law categorically states, "Evidence may be excluded if it is obtained in a manner that contravenes a Charter right and if its admission would bring the administration of justice into disrepute."

When the Alberta Court of Appeal ruling came down in 1995, Ryan Love's dripping nose assumed its place in Canadian legal history. Trevor McDonald, of the University of Manitoba's Faculty of Law, wrote a summary of the importance of DNA entitled *Genetic Justice: DNA Evidence and the Criminal Law in Canada*. The very first words of his argument centred on Ryan Love and his mucus-stained tissue. McDonald quoted Justice J.A. Kerans, one of Love's Alberta Court of Appeal judges, who said, "DNA evidence is the most dramatic forensic evidence ever discovered," as the appeal court reaffirmed Ryan Jason Love's second-degree murder conviction.

But the court's ruling revealed that Younggren had come within a whisker of freeing Love. The appeal court agreed with the lawyer that the scam the RCMP had earlier used to pull some of Love's hair out of his head for the DNA hair sample had violated his Charter rights, and that the "trickery, deceit, and bad faith employed by the police made this a serious and unnecessary Charter breach." The ruling continued, "The accused had not consented to allow an agent of the state to remove his hair, and this constituted an unreasonable search and seizure. The Court concludes that the DNA results from the hair samples should have been excluded."

That left only the tissue evidence. And this time the appeal court ruled against Younggren. Picking up a discarded tissue didn't violate anyone's rights. "The facts leading to the seizure of the discarded tissue would not generate revulsion amongst right-thinking Canadians," said the ruling. Therefore, the tissue sample itself "was sufficient to support a conviction" and what's more, to exclude it as evidence would have brought the administration of justice into disrepute.

Love's conviction had hung on one thin piece of Kleenex, and it held, which was only right and proper as it turned out. Love later wrote a long and apparently contrite and remorseful letter to Calgary newspaper columnist John Gradon, admitting, "Through my selfish actions I murdered a woman who did nothing to provoke me." Remember, Love spent more than two years evading police to stay out of jail, then pleaded not guilty, forcing his victim's family to suffer the ordeal of the trial. Even after being convicted, he still fought to squirm out of the prison sentence with lengthy, vain appeals that went as far as the Supreme Court of Canada. Only after all that had failed—with 20 years in prison looming ahead of him—did he suddenly confess and apparently become remorseful and full of contrition.

Columnist John Gradon saw through his cunning, manipulative effort. He wrote in his Calgary newspaper, "Why is it I just can't shake the image of Ryan Love swearing to his complete rehabilitation and final acceptance of guilt at a future parole hearing—and producing a copy of his letter to me as evidence of it?"

Thanks in part to Love's Kleenex case, the law of Canada was changed so police would never again have to resort to trickery, deceit and bad faith to obtain their DNA samples. On July 13, 1995, legislation was enacted giving police the legal right to take blood and hair samples from suspects for DNA analysis, if they have reasonable grounds to do so.

7

Three Deadly Desperadoes

LUCILLE ZELLER WAS INSIDE HER small family gas station in sleepy Exshaw, where the prairies of Alberta fade into the foothills of the Rocky Mountains, listening to the wireless. Two cops had been shot dead, way east on the prairies somewhere, and the fugitive gunmen—three of them—were thought to be driving west in a stolen, unmarked RCMP car with plate number MB 29–812. Lucille raised her head and looked out the window at three rough-looking guys at the pumps. "Oh God," she thought. "That's the car! MB 29–812."

She rushed out to warn her husband, Roy, who was at the pump. But before she got Roy's attention, the men drove off, heading farther west towards Banff. Even before Lucille opened her mouth, her husband told her that there was something suspicious about the three men. They had only asked for one gallon of gas, a very unusual request. It was 7:30 p.m. on October 7, 1935. Thoroughly shaken, Roy called the RCMP in Banff.

For the past two days, the fugitives had been running undetected across the prairies, from the Manitoba–Saskatchewan border to the edge of the Rockies. Roy's phone call put the RCMP back on their trail.

It all began when three masked men attempted an armed robbery at the Fawcett and Smith General Store in Benito, a tiny prairie town in Manitoba, almost on the Saskatchewan border. After pistol-whipping the storeowner, they made their getaway in an open touring car.

Three little villages sit slightly separated in a row along Highway 49, with Benito to the east, Arran in the middle and Pelley to the west. The border between the two provinces cuts Highway 49 between Benito and Arran, and you can drive through all three towns in just a few minutes.

Soon after midnight, in the first few minutes of October 5, the town constable of Benito, Constable William Wainwright, was on patrol with his partner, Constable John Shaw, of the Swan River RCMP detachment in Manitoba. They were in Shaw's unmarked RCMP car when they stopped the open touring car carrying the three men and discovered it was an unlicensed vehicle. It was a trivial traffic violation, and after checking the identities of the men, the two officers let them drive away. The three in the car were young men, sons of first-generation Doukhobor immigrants. They were Joe Posnikoff, 20, John Kalmakoff, 21, and Peter Woiken, 17.

Shortly after releasing the three, Constable Wainwright and Constable Shaw realized that the men they'd just let slip through their fingers were almost certainly the bandits who'd held up the Benito store at gunpoint. The two officers immediately set off along Highway 49 to try to catch up to the vehicle again. Soon after 4 a.m., they found it on a back street in Arran, where their robbery suspects had obviously been enjoying themselves at the local dance. A fourth man, Paul Bugero, as well as two girls from the dance, had joined them. This time, the officers arrested the three men, leaving Paul Bugero and the girls in Arran to drive home in the open touring car.

Neglecting to search their suspects, the policemen bundled Posnikoff, Kalmakoff and Woiken into the back of the unmarked RCMP car. Once everyone was settled, Constable Shaw, with Constable Wainwright sitting beside him in the passenger seat, started the car and drove through the back streets of Arran, heading out to Highway 49. The plan was to take all three suspects to the Pelley police station.

Suddenly, one of the suspects pulled out a bayonet blade and attacked Constable Wainwright, slashing violently at his head and neck. The other two suspects joined in, and in the confines of the car, Wainwright was overpowered. One of the men ripped the officer's 38-calibre revolver away from him and shot him in the head. Another pulled his own concealed gun out and blasted Shaw three times in the back of the head at point-blank range. The police car careened off the road and into the ditch, but none of the suspects in the back seat was injured.

They quickly dragged the two dead police officers out of the car. Woiken ripped Shaw's signet ring off his finger and took his handcuffs. The men then removed Wainwright's police belt and star, stripped Shaw of his uniform and took $230 from the officers' pockets. After sliding the officers' bodies into a slough in a farmer's field alongside the road, the threesome pushed the bloodstained police car out of the ditch and drove away in it.

Their attempts at a getaway became one long series of lunatic blunders; amazingly, none led to their capture. No one had seen them murder the officers, and no one would even miss the two cops for at least a few hours, so there was no need to race away. Very calmly, the three men embarked on a brazen plan of escape. With Wainwright's gun, all three of them were now armed. They had one entire uniform and another police belt, so they decided to pretend they were police officers and to talk their way out of the area. At 10:30 a.m.—more than five hours after the killings—they called at the farm of William Perepeluk, which was located just up the road from the murder scene. The farmer invited the three men to eat at his table. He noticed that they were all armed and that Woiken was wearing a police uniform and flashing a police belt. This seemed a little bizarre to Perepeluk, who recognized Posnikoff, Kalmakoff and Woiken from the community.

Apparently, the young men didn't realize they'd been recognized, because they told the farmer they were detectives hunting the murderer of two policemen who'd been killed nearby. Naturally, Perepeluk hadn't heard about the crime. No one had. As for being detectives, well, they were acting more like crazy men. They guzzled from a big jar of bootleg whisky and waved their guns around, laughing loudly and joking with each other. When they finished their meal, the three "detectives" told their host they were heading south into the United States where, they claimed, the murderer had fled. As they drove away, they misjudged the first bend in the road and rolled the RCMP car on its side. No matter. Another helpful farmer stopped and helped them right it and get on their way.

The men made two more stops on their puzzling getaway. First they each went home to their respective farms to pick up extra clothes. Then they went to a wedding reception and dance. After the dance they finally left the area, heading west. Hour after hour they travelled across the prairies, leaving Saskatchewan and pressing onward through the wheat fields of Alberta.

Early on October 7, a Doukhobor community farmer by the name of John Kollenchuk was ploughing with his team of horses in his field alongside Highway 49 between Arran and

Pelley. His horses suddenly shied and stopped dead in their tracks. The farmer looked around to see what had spooked them and quickly discovered the corpses of constables Wainwright and Shaw in the nearby slough. It was a shocking discovery that sparked front-page headlines across Canada. Prominent in the news stories were the descriptions of the three "desperate Doukhobor suspects" and of the unmarked RCMP vehicle they'd stolen as a getaway car. Radio stations across the prairies immediately began broadcasting the descriptions of the men and the car—and that's how Lucille Zeller came to hear it on the 7:30 p.m. news bulletin, just as the fugitives stopped at her husband's gas station.

Immediately after receiving Zeller's call, four Banff RCMP officers piled into one car and headed towards the Banff National Park gate, hoping to intercept the bandits. In the RCMP cruiser were Sergeant Thomas Wallace, Constable George "Scotty" Harrison, Constable Gray Campbell and Constable George "Nipper" Combe. When they reached the gate at the eastern end of the national park, they discovered that the stolen cruiser had already been there. The three men inside the car had refused to pay the park entrance fee and had turned around and headed east, back towards Calgary.

Meanwhile, Roy Zeller, the Exshaw gas station owner, had also called the Canmore RCMP. Constable John (Jack) Bonner took the call and learned which way the three killers were heading. He decided to drive straight out to the highway to see if he could intercept them. Constable Bonner picked up Canmore magistrate Robert Hawke on the way.

By this time, the fugitives were indeed desperate. To start with, they were almost penniless. In Exshaw they'd only had enough cash between them for one gallon of gas, and now their stolen police car was running on fumes. They didn't even have the two dollars required to get into the park. Realizing they needed to pull off another robbery in order to get more money, they turned around, headed back towards the park gate, and pulled over to the side of the road with the intention of robbing the occupants of the first car that came along.

A Calgary businessman, C. Thomas Scott, and his wife were heading for Banff and saw three men waving flashlights beside their apparently broken-down car. The couple stopped to help, and within seconds they were staring down the barrels of two revolvers. The men demanded money. They took $10 from Scott's pocket, but missed another $85 he'd hurriedly stuffed under the seat of the car when the guns had come out. The three young bandits were hopeless robbers. At one point, they snatched Scott's pocket watch, but when he promised not to report them to the police, they gave it back. Then they decided the best way to get through the park gate was to let the couple drive through ahead, and they'd scoot through immediately behind them.

In a bizarre twist of fate, Constable Bonner and Magistrate Hawke witnessed the whole robbery. It turned out that when they headed west from Canmore to intercept the bandits, Bonner had accurately anticipated where the stolen car would be. He and Hawke saw it parked a short distance ahead, moments before the Calgary couple drove up. Unaware that the bandits were waiting to ambush the next car that came along, Bonner and Hawke decided to pull over and keep an eye on the vehicle. As they watched the Calgary couple being robbed at gunpoint, helpless to intervene, they suddenly realized the implication of their own situation. If they hadn't stopped where they did, their car would have been the next car along, and they would have driven straight into an ambush. Bonner and Hawke took a few moments to gather their wits, then followed the now-moving Calgary couple and the fugitives, who were driving close behind.

Inevitably, on this cold and miserable night in October, the opening scene for a deadly gun battle was rapidly unfolding. The first four Banff RCMP officers had parked farther west of all three vehicles, intending to stop every car that came along from the east. Heading straight toward them was the car carrying Thomas Scott and his wife, followed a few seconds later by the armed men. Scott couldn't believe his luck. He'd just been robbed at gunpoint, and here were the police, just when he needed them. As he drove up he shouted, "The bandit car is right behind me!" and Constable Combe quickly waved him through.

Sergeant Wallace and Constable Harrison stepped onto

the road to stop the suspects' car. Blinded by its headlights, they were helpless as gunfire suddenly erupted from inside the stolen vehicle. The fugitives had opened fire through the windshield, instantly dropping Harrison with a bullet to the throat. As he went down, Harrison managed to shoot out the car's headlights, but the bandits ran their front wheels over him. He was now mortally wounded by gunfire and pinned under one of the car's wheels. Sergeant Wallace got off a few shots, and then had to run back to the police car for more ammunition. He returned to the gun battle and was immediately hit in the chest. He went down as well. The almighty gun battle shattered the still of the night.

Leaping from the car, the fugitives ran into deep brush at the side of the road under a barrage of bullets from the other two officers—Campbell and Combe. In a moment of great heroism, Campbell and Combe ran out from their cover— amid a hail of bullets—to pull their wounded partners to safety. Combe leaped into the bandits' car and reversed it off Harrison's body, and Campbell dragged Harrison into the police car.

At that moment, the RCMP car carrying Bonner and Hawke screeched onto the scene. Once the two wounded officers were safely in the police car, Campbell drove them at high speed the short distance to Canmore Hospital, in a desperate attempt to save their lives.

Meanwhile, the gunfire persisted. Two of the fugitives had fled the area, but the third was hiding somewhere in the nearby bushes, firing at the three remaining law officers, who were trying to take cover behind tree stumps and fallen logs.

After dropping Harrison and Wallace off at the hospital, Constable Campbell returned to the scene and joined Combe in a search south of the road. The Canmore pair, Constable Bonner and Magistrate Hawke, searched to the north. Suddenly, Combe saw a slight movement in the bushes. He shone his flashlight and spotted one of the men crouched on one knee, carefully aiming a revolver. Combe shot him in the head, killing him instantly. Joe Posnikoff was the first of the desperadoes to die. He was later found to have four police bullets in him. He'd obviously been hit in the first exchange, before Combe finished him off. When Combe and Campbell rolled his body over, they saw that he was clutching the police special 38-calibre revolver that had belonged to Benito town constable William Wainwright.

Word was sent back to the Banff and Canmore RCMP detachments. There had been a terrible gun battle. Two officers had been horribly wounded and were clinging to life in hospital after being transferred from Canmore to Calgary. One fugitive had been shot dead, but two others had escaped.

Reinforcements were sent immediately. RCMP officers flooded in to boost the manhunt, accompanied by many Banff and Canmore citizen volunteers. The volunteers were given rifles, and teams of men threw a dragnet around the area between the Banff National Park gate and Canmore. As heavy snow began to fall, searchers kept their eyes on every trail through the forest. The railway tracks were also guarded, and police patrolled the main highway. All through the night the hunt went on, but still the two fugitives remained at large.

The next morning, the rest of Alberta learned of the gun battle when the October 8 *Calgary Albertan* devoted its entire front page to the story, under a rarely used five-tier headline:

TWO ALBERTA MOUNTIES SHOT,
MAN KILLED IN CANMORE HUNT

GUNMEN WHO FIRED ON POLICE CONNECTED
WITH SASKATCHEWAN SLAYINGS

Sergeant Wallace, Constable Harrison victims
of gunmen's bullets in serious condition

WIDESPREAD HUNT UNDERWAY

Dead man identified as one of trio wanted
in Saskatchewan double murder

At 6:45 a.m., just as people were reading their early morning paper, a heavier pall of gloom descended on the searchers. Word came through that Sergeant Wallace had died in hospital of his gunshot wounds.

The search intensified. Then, civilian volunteers Jack White and Ed Thompson spotted the fugitives out on the snowy road. They drove hurriedly to the Banff National Park gate and reported what they'd seen to park warden Bill Neish and volunteer Harry Leacock. Both men had been deputized as police for the manhunt. Neish was very much the man for the job. He'd served in the army overseas in the First World War and was also a former Royal Northwest Mounted Police officer and a former member of the Alberta Provincial Police.

All four men immediately piled into a car, returned to the area and searched again in even heavier snow. This time, they found nothing. The civilian volunteers White and Thompson drove into Banff to tell police they thought they'd seen the fugitives. Neish and Leacock stayed behind and patrolled the area of the sighting on foot. This time they saw fresh tracks in the new snow. They were about to follow the footprints when two vehicles carrying more volunteers pulled up with urgent news. The two fugitives had been spotted farther west along the road. Neish and Leacock commandeered a passing car owned by a civilian named Ed McBride. With McBride driving and Neish and Leacock riding on the outside of the car clinging to the running boards, they headed west into the snowstorm.

In a few minutes, they saw the two fugitives scrambling up a slope through the snow. They shouted to the killers to put up their hands, but instead of a surrender, another gun battle broke out. One of the killers turned and fired at Neish. The bullet whistled over his head. Keeping cool under fire, Neish, a noted marksman, hit the gunman with two bullets from his .303 rifle. The gunman dropped. Neish heard the man scream in pain and fired again. The gunman was silent. The second fugitive ran deeper into the forest and took cover behind a fallen log. Neish instantly saw the barrel of the man's rifle. Neish fired again, and the killer's body contorted violently as he was hit. He then lay still.

Neish and Leacock were cautiously approaching the two fugitives when police reinforcements, alerted by the renewed gunfire, joined them. Together, Neish, Leacock and the rest of the police surrounded the two gunmen. They were both badly wounded—each had taken two bullets to the stomach. "Got them both," said Neish.

The next moment made RCMP history. Calgary RCMP sergeant Jack Cawsey had been following the bandits through the snow with his tracker dog, Dale. The dog's skills had led Cawsey to the shooting scene at the moment of the last shot. It was the first time ever that an RCMP tracker dog had been used to hunt fugitives, and Dale performed perfectly. On hearing the last shot fired, he leaped to attack the gunman. Unfortunately, the shooter was Deputy William Neish. Sergeant Cawsey instantly ordered the dog to release Neish. In seconds, the dog was guarding the wounded Kalmakoff until the police had him under control. Next, Dale stood watch over the other wounded man, Woiken, until he too was under police control. The car belonging to civilian Ed McBride was then used to carry the two wounded gunmen to the Banff Mineral Springs Hospital.

It had been a devastating and tragic evening. At 5:50 p.m., word came from the Calgary hospital that Constable Harrison had died from his gunshot wounds. The bullet that hit him in the throat had smashed his spinal column and ricocheted inside his body, puncturing a lung. From the hospital in Banff came word that the last two fugitives had also died of their gunshot wounds. The two gun battles in Banff National Park had left five men dead, and the total death toll since the gunmen had first made their bolt for freedom across the prairies was seven. Four of the dead were police officers. The story brought another shocking headline in the *Calgary Albertan* on October 9:

TWO POLICEMEN, THREE BANDITS DIE
FROM WOUNDS IN ALBERTA

BAND OF DESPERADOES WIPED OUT IN ALBERTA,
YOUNG CONSTABLE DIES

It was one of the blackest incidents law enforcement in Canada had ever experienced. Glowing testimonials were made about the two Banff Mounties, Sergeant Thomas Wallace and Constable George Harrison. Both officers were buried with full military honours, with thousands of people paying their respects. Back in Swan River, Manitoba, Constable John Shaw was also buried with a full military funeral, as was Constable William Wainwright in Benito. So many people crammed into the tiny church in Benito that the floor began to sag and was in danger of collapsing. Only when everyone trooped carefully outside could the service be carried out.

The three murderers had far more humble burials. John Kalmakoff's parents took his body home and buried him in an unmarked grave in a wheat field on their farm. Peter Woiken's family members, especially his father, Harry, were distraught when they heard the news that Woiken was dead. Ashamed when they learned how much grief he had brought to other families, they nevertheless wanted to take his body home to Arran for burial. However, they were poor farmers and simply couldn't afford the cost. They never did claim his body.

Joe Posnikoff's parents, Mary and George, travelled all the way to Banff to take one last look at their son, but they returned home to Saskatchewan without his body. Some reports say they were too poor to have his remains sent home. But other people, those the Posnikoff family had talked to out west, were convinced that Posnikoff had brought such shame on his family that they disowned him. Perhaps it was a combination of the two. Whatever the reason, the Posnikoffs also did not claim their son's body.

Banff and Canmore authorities were now faced with

a dilemma. Where would they bury the bodies of Joe Posnikoff and Peter Woiken? Residents of both towns, who had poured out their grief and sorrow at the funerals of the murdered police officers, had no such feelings for the officers' killers. And they let their opinions be known. The authorities soon bowed to public pressure and refused to allow either Posnikoff or Woiken to be buried in the towns' cemeteries, which left only the sacred burial grounds in the Wesley Cemetery on the Stoney Indian Reservation between Exshaw and Cochrane. But the Stoneys also refused to have the bodies buried in sacred ground. Finally, they relented somewhat and allowed the bodies to be buried just outside their cemetery.

Worried about possible public reaction, the authorities kept the burials secret. Only a clergyman, a funeral director and a gravedigger were at the site as Joseph Posnikoff and Peter Woiken were buried together in the same grave. When the three men left after the barest of services, only a small mound of stones and rocks marked the spot where the two killers had been laid to rest.

8

A Killer's Happy Birthday Treat

IT'S NOT EVERY DAY A murderer and prison escapee leaves such uproar and outrage in his wake that he sparks a new call for the death penalty, causes heads to roll in the nation's prison system, and his name reaches the very corridors of power in Ottawa. But convicted triple murderer Daniel Gingras did all that and more. The creation of such chaos required a hidden depth of evil and an environment in which it could flourish. Gingras was the necessary embodiment of evil, and those in the justice system in Edmonton handed him a golden opportunity to wreak his havoc on society. Even before Gingras first landed in jail in Edmonton's maximum security institution, his appalling record of violent crime was far worse than most criminals amass in their whole lifetime—and he had only just started.

We pick up his life of violence in the middle of a dramatic gunfight with the cops in Montreal in 1974, when he was fleeing after holding up a fur store at gunpoint. Police intercepted him and shot him twice, but he survived. He was convicted of armed robbery and sentenced to 10 years in prison, which he served in the medium-security penitentiary at Cowansville, Quebec. On November 11, 1978, he escaped. Weeks later, on December 16, this escape cost an innocent man his life. Gingras was on the lam for another month before being arrested on January 21, 1979, with his brother, Claude, and charged with murdering the innocent man, Yves Richer.

Seven months later, in August 1979, Daniel Gingras pleaded guilty to 10 charges, including the horrific second-degree murder of Richer. The court heard Gingras forced his victim onto the floor of a stolen car and executed him by shooting him in the back of the head with a sawed-off 20-gauge shotgun. For this "cowardly vicious act" Judge Rushton Lamb sentenced Gingras to life imprisonment with no possibility of parole for 12 years. In sentencing him, the judge added some uncomfortably prophetic words: "In your case it is the opinion of the Court that there is very little possibility of rehabilitation." By all accounts, Judge Lamb's opinion wasn't passed on to the prison and parole authorities.

Montreal police had strong suspicions Gingras may have been linked to an even worse crime—a double murder of two sisters. This had occurred during the two months he was on the run, but he was never charged in connection with the case. Gingras and his brother had met two women, Solange Jalbert, 18, and her elder sister Céline, 20, soon after Christmas 1978 at a nightclub, and during early January the women stayed periodically at the Gingras' apartment. Four days before Gingras was arrested for the shotgun murder, the two sisters were found strangled to death in their apartment. Montreal police pursued the Gingras brothers as their prime suspects, but no charges were ever laid, no other suspects were ever found, and the double slaying remains unsolved to this day.

Gingras started his 1979 life sentence in Montreal, but by 1985 he had earned such a reputation as a prison "rat" for informing on fellow prisoners that he was transferred for his own safety to the Edmonton maximum-security prison. With this move, prison authorities successfully protected Gingras from those around him. But who would protect society from Gingras? The prison authorities certainly didn't. It was later revealed that Gingras the master manipulator had become once again a star informant for two years at Edmonton, receiving perks for his inside work. The stage was set for disaster.

June 29, 1987, was Gingras' 36th birthday, and it seemed he was due for another perk after he'd recently ratted on a fellow prisoner. This time his reward was to be a pass out of jail for a day's shopping at the busy West Edmonton Mall. He would have to be escorted, naturally. The prison authorities, who first planned to have Gingras handcuffed to an armed 220-pound guard for the day, let him choose who he wanted instead and entrusted him to a 52-year-old unarmed social worker.

The implications of this were shocking. Gingras was a violent career criminal and convicted killer who had executed a man in cold blood after escaping from prison once before. His additional criminal record tallied 34 convictions, including six armed robberies, and a sentencing judge had warned he would never change his ways. This man was being let out into Edmonton's most populated and sprawling building, thronging with thousands of shoppers, with only an unarmed social worker standing between him and freedom.

The prison's security chiefs vigorously opposed the pass, but were overruled. Regulations forbidding such passes to prisoners like Gingras were ignored, and files detailing Gingras' full violent background weren't passed to the National Parole Board, which approved the pass. Finally, the guards who saw him about to leave the front gate of the prison refused to let him out, certain a terrible mistake had been made. They checked and were told to let him through. Even then, they still wrote "AWOL" in the log alongside his name.

Gingras, the birthday boy, wasn't inside West Edmonton Mall a few minutes before he overpowered his social worker and disappeared into the crowds of shoppers. Now all Canada was at his mercy. After a quick foray to Quebec, Gingras soon travelled back to Edmonton by Via Rail train in early August 1987 with a friend, Joseph Jean Vital Piquette, a rodeo clown and the son of a police chief.

The threat to the community became more dire when Gingras teamed up with another man, Calvin Harvey Smoker, then aged 40, an accused murderer who didn't have to escape from prison. He was let out on $5,000 bail without even having to put down a deposit. The attorney general's department had been shocked that an Edmonton judge gave bail to a man charged with first-degree murder and was appealing the decision to the Alberta Court of Appeal. But it was too late; Gingras and Smoker were now running together.

After several days in Edmonton, Gingras decided he could use Piquette's identification papers to help him spring another convict out of jail for a fat fee. He invited the rodeo clown to a barbeque at the home of a prostitute where he was staying. On August 12, while Smoker watched, he executed Piquette, putting four bullets in him: one in the head, two in the back and one in the chest. Then he took the body and dumped it in a ditch in Edmonton, surprisingly near the prison from which he was still a fugitive.

The next day, Gingras moved south to Medicine Hat,

where he and Smoker planned some armed robberies of supermarkets, for which they would need a getaway car. It was the terrible misfortune of 24-year-old Medicine Hat resident Wanda Lee Woodward, an auto upholsterer, to be in the wrong place at the wrong time as she came out of the city's Southview Mall. As she was about to get into her truck, Gingras decided it would make the perfect vehicle for their crime spree. She was hit on the head, knocked unconscious and bundled into her own truck, and the two men drove off with her. It was August 14, and an agonizing nightmare for Wanda's family began. They had no idea where she was, or if she was alive or dead.

Gingras, meanwhile, had stores to rob. He didn't need this "woman nuisance," as he described her, so he bound her hands and feet, tied her shoelaces together and strangled her with them. Then he drove 20 kilometres south of Medicine Hat and dumped her body. All this diversion had wasted a little time in the two men's busy day, but their plan was soon back on track. By 8 p.m. they were holding up a Medicine Hat Safeway store at gunpoint. Gingras threatened one cashier with his gun and pointed it at a woman customer in the parking lot as the men escaped in Woodward's truck with $900.

Alberta was paying a high price for Gingras' birthday present. On August 16, Piquette's body was discovered in the Edmonton ditch, and the next day Woodward's truck was found abandoned in a gravel pit three kilometres south of Medicine Hat. There was no sign of Wanda or more than $300 she'd withdrawn at the mall just before she disappeared. The nightmare for Leslie Woodward and his family worsened with the finding of his daughter's truck.

By now it was time for Gingras to move on again. Late on August 21, as he travelled north towards Fort St. John with a couple of prostitutes in a stolen car, he ran smack into an RCMP roadblock at Grand Cache and was recaptured. Five days later, Wanda's body was discovered where Gingras had dumped it, and the Woodward family's anguish reached its depths.

Gingras and Smoker were charged with the two murders in Edmonton and Medicine Hat, and the now familiar wheels of justice revolved around them both in a new string of hearings and trials. For the first time, the whole of Alberta began to learn about the disastrous decisions that had led to this double tragedy, and the first small cries of outrage over Gingras' escape were heard.

The first clue that serious errors in judgment had been made came when Solicitor General James Kelleher announced that the warden at Edmonton, prison boss Sepp Tschierschwitz, was gone. He'd been "relieved of his post" and farmed out to a Saskatchewan prison where he was to deal with nothing more controversial than planning and resource management. What's more, said Kelleher, internal inquiries weren't complete, and more heads could roll in the future. A few details trickled out even before Gingras got to trial. In March 1988, it was revealed that critical prison files detailing the dangers posed by Gingras were withheld from the National Parole Board as it made its decision to approve his infamous day pass. Many people wanted to know why.

So much publicity had surrounded the Woodward murder case in Medicine Hat that it was decided to move the trial to Calgary. In October 1988, the trial opened in the city's Court of Queen's Bench, and Gingras pleaded not guilty. It lasted nearly three weeks, but in the end the jury took less than two hours to convict Gingras of first-degree murder. By law, the jury members had been told nothing of Gingras' past. After pronouncing him guilty, they were astounded to hear of his violent record that included the previous murder in Quebec. On November 16, 1988, Justice Allen Sulatycky handed down the mandatory life sentence with no parole for 25 years, advising the parole board 25 years hence against letting Gingras out even then. The conviction was seen as official confirmation that the blunder of letting a convicted murderer out of prison on a day pass had cost an innocent woman her life. It opened up a flood of public outrage.

Wanda's father, Leslie Woodward, speaking from the family home in Irvine, a village just outside Medicine Hat, echoed the judge's warning that Gingras should never be let out of prison again. "I hope he never gets out because he'll do it again. I'm sure he has no feelings for anybody, for anybody's life at all," he said. "Not a minute of my life goes by that I don't think of her. It should never have happened."

Wanda's mother, Evelyn, who was pleased justice had been served by the conviction, said the pain of losing her daughter would never be erased.

Wanda's murder sparked an instant call to bring back hanging in Canada. Medicine Hat MP Bob Porter, whose daughter was a personal friend of Wanda, said Gingras should have been hanged. "I would have no qualms in voting for capital punishment in a case like that of Gingras. This was first-degree murder, premeditated murder," he said. Other proponents of the death penalty echoed his opinion.

Alberta Bow River Tory MP Gordon Taylor predicted more innocent people would die because killers weren't being executed. "Murderers like Gingras are laughing at the people of Canada, especially at the bleeding hearts who want to continue to molly-coddle killers," he said. "The sad part is a lot more innocent people are going to die because some MPs won't listen to what a majority of their constituents want—the return of capital punishment."

Wanda's murder also sparked an immediate and frantic campaign against any convicted murderer being let out of prison on a day pass in future. Victims of Violence, an Edmonton-based lobby group for the families of violent crime victims, organized 10,000 letters to the solicitor general urging that day passes for convicted killers be banned. "If there is no capital punishment for killers, then life sentences must mean life," said the group's founder,

Gary Rosenfeldt. "Society doesn't owe it to murderers to let them out on birthday treat day passes, and we want the system changed."

In the spring of 1989, the repercussions of letting a convicted killer out of jail were multiplied when an Edmonton Court of Queen's Bench jury found Gingras guilty of the second-degree murder of Vital Piquette. One witness told the jury Gingras had boasted in jail how he killed Piquette for his identification papers, in what he called "an even trade." Gingras told the inmate, "I got his papers, he got my bullets." And the prosecution had an eyewitness—Calvin Harvey Smoker, who turned on Gingras in a deal with the Crown. Smoker, facing a first-degree murder rap in Piquette's killing, agreed to plead guilty to being an accessory after the fact to the murder of Piquette, with a promise the Crown would recommend he only serve three months in jail. In return, he told the jury he sat in a car and watched Gingras pull the trigger and shoot Piquette to death. At a later hearing, the first-degree murder charge against Smoker in the Woodward murder was reduced, but he was sentenced to three years in jail after being convicted of the unlawful confinement of Woodward and being an accessory to her murder.

After Gingras had been convicted of both murders, the floodgates of anger were flung open. Gingras stirred the pot himself when he persuaded prison authorities to plan a trip for him to the Royal Alexandra Hospital in Edmonton for plastic surgery on self-inflicted wrist injuries. Then he bragged that he would use the visit to escape again. The trip was cancelled when the escape bid was publicized.

The federal government announced an independent inquiry into the tragedy headed by Edmonton lawyer John Weir, but then infuriated some Alberta MPs by insisting it be held behind closed doors. Calgary Northeast Tory MP Alex Kindy said, "I am very upset. This is no good. The public has a right to know all the facts." Edmonton East New Democrat MP Ross Harvey said the government was leaving itself open to claims of whitewashing.

When Weir's report was published on December 20, 1989, its condemnation of the prison authorities was disturbing. Gingras was a dangerous criminal who never should have been released on a day pass, it said, and it laid the blame at the feet of the warden, Sepp Tschierschwitz, and the prison corrections operation co-ordinator, Fred Perrin. The report recommended both men should be retired early.

But the biggest furor was caused by the whole sections blacked out by government censors before the report was released. What the government had made public was bad enough, and now everyone was demanding to know how damning the censored material was. Attorney General Ken Rostad announced that the province of Alberta was looking into the possibility of bringing criminal charges against the prison officials who'd let Gingras out. Scott Newark, the Wetaskiwin, Alberta, prosecutor who spearheaded the campaign to get the independent inquiry in the first place, was livid. He was so angry that what he called "devastating" information had been kept secret by the government censors that he threatened to blow the lid off the case and make public the report's secret sections.

As the major row boiled in Alberta and Ottawa, a quiet little episode was played out in a Saskatchewan backwater tucked away from the action, where Tschierschwitz had been sent as punishment. Now he and Fred Perrin were given early retirement, fulfilling two of the recommendations in the Weir report. But even kicking Tschierschwitz out of the correctional system altogether didn't appease Newark. "That deal's just a golden handshake," he said.

Prosecutor Newark made good his threat to reveal some of the secrets blacked out by the government in Weir's report. He told the House of Commons justice committee that one blacked-out passage concluded the prison warden had been "wilfully negligent" in releasing Gingras. Spurred on by Newark, the committee now demanded of the government and Corrections Canada that the full, unedited report be made public, with all its revelations about what really happened during the scandal. But Corrections Canada and Canada's solicitor general dug their heels in, claiming privacy and security reasons. Few people bought this explanation, as everyone believed they had embarrassing secrets to hide.

By October 1990, the Commons justice committee was planning to subpoena the government into handing over the full unexpurgated version of the report. The scandal dragged on into 1991, until a parliamentary lawyer said the report must be released because Parliament was exempt from the Privacy Act. Finally, after a year-long battle, the persistence of the justice committee was rewarded when its members got to study the full report, including the secret sections Corrections Canada had fought so hard to conceal. The committee still wasn't permitted to reveal the details to the public, but the facts did come out, thanks largely to a series of newspaper articles by *Edmonton Journal* reporter Tom Barrett, who had contacts who leaked him the inside story.

It was a shocker. Weir's report revealed officials knew Gingras was planning escapes in 1986 and 1987, right up to six weeks before they let him out on the infamous day pass. Weir had discovered that vital documents had disappeared from Gingras' file. One officer, who wrote an official report on overhearing Gingras discussing an escape plan, found later his report was missing. Other guards who filed internal charges against Gingras were surprised no action was taken on the charges and that their paperwork had also disappeared from the file.

Weir found that three prison profile books describing Gingras as a "major escape risk" to be let out only in handcuffs and leg irons had all vanished after the escape. Weir knew these items had gone only by interviewing the officers who'd put them in the file in the first place. Weir also had interviewed officers who couldn't believe Gingras was being let out and who warned senior officials up the line about the terrible risk they'd be taking. The senior officials said they'd passed on the warning to prison warden Tschierschwitz, but he denied ever being told.

Weir found that Tschierschwitz and Perrin had had many private sessions with Gingras, often in "the hole," the prison's segregation unit. One of the sections originally blacked out by government censors covered an incident when Gingras was discovered with three illegal drill bits in his cell, for which he was thrown in the hole. But before the scheduled disciplinary hearing was called, Tschierschwitz released Gingras from the hole and no hearing ever took place. "No explanation is given for this, nor is there any explanation as to why the charge was not proceeded with or otherwise disposed of," wrote Weir. It was just one of many incidents Corrections Canada obviously never wanted exposed to the light of day.

Weir found that prison staff who recognized Gingras as a hardened criminal and major escape risk were taken off his case and replaced. The convict was manipulating the system in order to get the case management officers he wanted around him. It had paid off. One officer of Gingras' choosing lied when he prepared the progress summary for the birthday day-pass application. Weir's report called the summary a "misleading and factually false document." The summary stated that all the staff on Gingras' case supported the application, but the other staff members hadn't been consulted at all, and had they been, they would have violently opposed it. One officer even considered Gingras "the most serious case" he'd ever seen at the Edmonton Institution. The summary also omitted to mention Gingras had murdered someone after an earlier prison escape. Next, Weir found that Tschierschwitz had failed to hold a formal board hearing to consider Gingras' application for a day pass, where all officers could have expressed their views. Such meetings were standard with any similar application at any prison. Tschierschwitz could offer Weir no explanation why he hadn't done this, and Weir's report was highly critical of this omission.

Weir's report said the actions of Fred Perrin were the most inexplicable. Perrin knew Gingras' file showed him to be involved in escape plots, drug dealing within the prison and other criminal activities. He even told Weir he had been warned days in advance Gingras was planning to escape if given the pass. What's more, Perrin told Weir he didn't doubt Gingras would try to escape, and if he did so, he'd "definitely be dangerous." Yet Perrin signed the pass, though later he tried to convince other staff members that someone had forged his signature.

After reading the shocking details in the full report for three hours, Tory MP Bob Horner, the Commons justice committee chairman, had one conclusion. "People should have been fired," he said. Although Tschierschwitz and Perrin were forced to take early retirement, no one was fired.

Meanwhile Gingras continued laughing at Canadians from inside his prison cell. On August 20, 1991, he was married in the special handling unit of Saskatchewan Penitentiary, the rings exchanged through holes in the prison wire barrier. His bride, Judy Maleki of Glendale, California, had fallen in love with the triple murderer when she saw his photograph in the *World Weekly News* supermarket tabloid newspaper. In an in-depth interview with *Calgary Sun* reporter Stuart Hunter, Maleki, who once appeared in the film *Night of the Living Dead Part Two*, described Gingras as her "ideal man" who wrote her letters and poetry every day. "Men have always treated me like a sex object because I'm good looking. Danny isn't like that," she said. "I know people probably think I'm crazy but I don't care what they think. All I care about is Danny."

The couple was denied a conjugal visit by the prison. Gingras becomes eligible for consideration for parole in 2013. If parole were granted then, he'd be sharing his honeymoon with a wife who would be 71 years old.

The marriage brought bitter resentment from Wanda Woodward's mother, Evelyn, as she and her husband continued their ongoing lawsuit, suing the government, the corrections service and prison officers in Edmonton for negligence in Wanda's murder. "Why should he be allowed to get married?" she asked. "He never gave my daughter a chance to get married."

In the end, the voices the Gingras case raised to bring

back hanging were stilled and capital punishment wasn't reinstated. Yet the controversy never fails to boil over again when violent criminals reoffend and innocents like Wanda Woodward and Vital Piquette pay the price. And there will always be unrepentant killers like Gingras who try to manipulate the justice and prison systems to their advantage.

After all, it is no mistake that he has a two-word tattoo engraved large across his back. It reads, "Murder Incorporated."

Further Reading

Anderson, Frank. *A Dance with Death: Canadian Women on the Gallows 1754–1954*. Saskatoon: Fifth House Ltd., 1996.

Anderson, Frank. *The Rum Runners*. Edmonton: Lone Pine Publishing, 1991.

Carpenter, Jock. *Bootlegger's Bride*. Canada: Gorman & Gorman, 1993.

Carter, David J. *Behind Canadian Barbed Wire*. Elkwater: Eagle Butte Press Ltd., 1980. Reprinted as *POW — Behind Canadian Barbed Wire*, 2004.

Gray, James H. *Talk to My Lawyer! Great Stories of Southern Alberta's Bar and Bench*. Edmonton: Hurtig Publishers Ltd., 1987.

Index

Acknowledgements

I would like to thank the numerous police officers across Alberta with whom I worked during my 16 years as a crime reporter with the *Calgary Sun*. They helped me with background information on many of the cases in this book. Most of these officers were with the Calgary Police Service. Especially, I want to thank all the "secret sources" among them, who have had to remain anonymous at all times. You know who you are!

To Calgary staff sergeant George Rocks, who was head of the homicide unit for years and never once lost patience with me bugging him for more information at all hours of the day and night, I thank you for all your help.

Thanks so much to my wife, Amanda, who has endured me talking about murders and dismemberments, and hangings and blood-spatterings, all the time I was writing the book. And thanks for allowing our house to be filled from study to attic with my murder files, notebooks and newspaper cuttings. Her computer skills have been invaluable at times in saving me when parts of the book were in danger of disappearing into cyberspace forever.

I am grateful for the constant help I received from Barbara Van Orden, the librarian at the Quadra Branch of the Vancouver Island Regional Library, who found every reference I needed in researching the book. My thanks also to Johnnie Bachusky, a fellow journalist and author, who steered me towards this book. I wish to thank my editor, Dianne Smyth, for reining me in when I was enthusiastically over-loquacious. She made this a better book to read.

About the Author

Peter B. Smith lives with his wife on Quadra Island, British Columbia, where he retired after a 37-year career as a newspaper crime reporter. He was the crime reporter for *The News* in Portsmouth, England, for 21 years, where he was on call with all three emergency services—fire, police and ambulance—covering thousands of stories of death and destruction. After immigrating to Canada in 1987, he was the crime reporter at the *Calgary Sun* for 16 years, retiring in 2003.

Peter has received numerous accolades, including awards for his coverage of the massacre at the Columbine High School in Littleton, Colorado. Peter also travelled to England to cover the story of Dr. Harold Shipman, the physician who murdered 216 of his patients.

To satisfy his two main interests in life, sea fishing and stamps, Peter ran a twice-weekly sea-angling column for 10 years in England and wrote more than 600 columns for stamp collectors in the *Calgary Sun*, spanning 13 years and earning a national Canadian philatelic literary award.

Peter's second Canadian true-crime book, *CSI Alberta: The Secrets of Skulls and Skeletons*, was published in 2009. His previous works include *Sea Angling in Southern England* and the official history of the Portsmouth (England) Fire Brigade, *Go To Blazes*, as well as a specialist stamp book called *Vanuatu's Postal History—The First Decade*. Peter is currently working on a history of the postal service, post offices and postmasters on the tiny islands around his Quadra Island home.

Don't stop at just one: there are many more great crime/mystery books to bring home and enjoy.

If you enjoyed *Prairie Murders*, look for these popular titles:

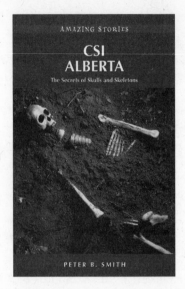

CSI Alberta:
The Secrets of
Skulls and Skeletons

Peter B. Smith

(ISBN 978-1-894974-84-4)

British Columbia Murders: Mysteries, Crimes and Scandals
Susan McNicoll
(ISBN 978-1-551539-63-8)

**Legends, Liars, and Lawbreakers: Incredible Tales
from the Pacific Northwest**
Valerie Green
(ISBN 978-1-551537-71-9)

Visit our online catalogue at www.heritagehouse.ca to see the entire list of books in this series.